First World War
and Army of Occupation
War Diary
France, Belgium and Germany

14 DIVISION
42 Infantry Brigade
Princess Louise's (Argyll & Sutherland Highlanders)
14th Battalion
1 April 1918 - 6 June 1919

WO95/1900/1

The Naval & Military Press Ltd
www.nmarchive.com
Published in association with The National Archives

Published by

The Naval & Military Press Ltd

Unit 10 Ridgewood Industrial Park,
Uckfield, East Sussex,
TN22 5QE England
Tel: +44 (0) 1825 749494

www.naval-military-press.com

www.nmarchive.com

This diary has been reprinted in facsimile from the original. Any imperfections are inevitably reproduced and the quality may fall short of modern type and cartographic standards.

© **Crown Copyright**
Images reproduced by permission of The National Archives, London, England, 2015.

Contents

Document type	Place/Title	Date From	Date To
Heading	WO95/1900/1 14 Div 42 Infantry Brigade 1918 Apr-1919 Jun 14th Battalion Argyll & Sutherland Highlanders		
Heading	14th Division 42nd Infy Bde 14th Bn A & S H. Apl 1918-Jun 1919 From 40 Div 120 Bde		
Miscellaneous			
Heading	War Diary Of The 14th. Battn. Argyll & Sutherland Highlanders For The Month Of April-1918 In The Field. 5th. May, 1918. Commanding 14th. Bn. A. & S.H.		
Miscellaneous			
War Diary	Fleurbaix Right Sub-Sector	01/04/1918	04/04/1918
War Diary	Sailly	05/04/1918	07/04/1918
War Diary	P Camp Poperinghe Area	08/04/1918	09/04/1918
Miscellaneous			
War Diary	Elverdinghe	10/04/1918	17/04/1918
War Diary	Brandhoek	18/04/1918	20/04/1918
War Diary	Buysscheure	21/04/1918	30/04/1918
Miscellaneous			
Heading	War Diary Of The 14th. Argyll & Sutherland Highlanders For The Month Of May-1918 (Volume XXIV) In The Field 5-6-18. Lieut. Colonel, Commanding 14th. Argyll & Sutherland Highlanders.		
Miscellaneous			
War Diary	Buysscheure	01/05/1918	09/05/1918
Miscellaneous			
War Diary	Buysscheure	10/05/1918	15/05/1918
War Diary	Woincourt	16/05/1918	16/05/1918
Miscellaneous			
War Diary	Gamaches	17/05/1918	17/05/1918
War Diary	La Haie	18/05/1918	24/05/1918
Miscellaneous			
War Diary	La Haie	25/05/1918	26/05/1918
War Diary	Mille Bosc	27/05/1918	31/05/1918
Miscellaneous			
War Diary	Appendix		
Miscellaneous			
Heading	90th Brigade. 80th Division. Battalion transferred to 14th Division 15.6.18 War Diary Of 14th Aug & Suth'd Highrs From 1-6-18 To 17-6-18 Volume No. 25		
Miscellaneous			
War Diary	Mille Bosc	01/06/1918	06/06/1918
Miscellaneous			
War Diary	Mille Bosc	07/06/1918	15/06/1918
Miscellaneous			
War Diary	Etaples	16/06/1918	16/06/1918
War Diary	Boulogne	17/06/1918	17/06/1918
Miscellaneous			
Heading	Volume XXVI War Diary Of The 14th Argyll & Sutherland Highlanders. For The Month Of July 1918		

Miscellaneous			
War Diary	Havre	03/07/1918	03/07/1918
War Diary	Boulogne	04/07/1918	04/07/1918
Miscellaneous			
War Diary	Boulogne	04/07/1918	05/07/1918
War Diary	Belle	06/07/1918	09/07/1918
Miscellaneous			
War Diary	Belle	10/07/1918	11/07/1918
War Diary	Boursin	12/07/1918	12/07/1918
War Diary	Hocquinghem	13/07/1918	13/07/1918
War Diary	Louches	14/07/1918	14/07/1918
Miscellaneous			
War Diary	Louches	15/07/1918	15/07/1918
War Diary	Nordausques	16/07/1918	19/07/1918
Miscellaneous			
War Diary	Nordausques	20/07/1918	24/07/1918
Miscellaneous			
War Diary	Nordausques	24/07/1918	28/07/1918
Miscellaneous			
War Diary	Nordausques	29/07/1918	29/07/1918
War Diary	Le Marais	30/07/1918	30/07/1918
War Diary	Nordpeene	31/07/1918	31/07/1918
Miscellaneous			
Heading	War Diary 14th Arg & Suth'd Highrs From 1-8-18 To 31-8-18 Vol 27		
Miscellaneous			
War Diary	St. Sylvestre Cappel	01/08/1918	04/08/1918
Miscellaneous			
War Diary	St. Sylvestre Cappel	05/08/1918	07/08/1918
Miscellaneous			
War Diary	St. Sylvestre Cappel	08/08/1918	10/08/1918
Miscellaneous			
War Diary	St Sylvestre Cappel	11/08/1918	12/08/1918
War Diary	Zudrove	13/08/1918	13/08/1918
War Diary	Bayenghem	14/08/1918	14/08/1918
Miscellaneous			
War Diary	Bayenghem	15/08/1918	19/08/1918
Miscellaneous			
War Diary	Louches	20/08/1918	22/08/1918
Miscellaneous			
War Diary	Louches	23/08/1918	23/08/1918
War Diary	Proven	24/08/1918	25/08/1918
Miscellaneous			
War Diary	Proven	25/08/1918	27/08/1918
Miscellaneous			
War Diary	Proven	28/08/1918	29/08/1918
War Diary	Siege Camp	30/08/1918	31/08/1918
Miscellaneous			
Heading	War Diary Of 14th Arg & Suth'd Highrs From 1-9-18 To 30-9-18 Volume No 28		
Miscellaneous			
War Diary	Siege Camp	01/09/1918	04/09/1918
Miscellaneous			
War Diary	Siege Camp	05/09/1918	05/09/1918
War Diary	Left Batt. Left Sub Sector Ypres	06/09/1918	08/09/1918
Miscellaneous			

War Diary	Left Batt. Left Sub Sector Ypres	09/09/1918	13/09/1918
War Diary	Dirty Bucket Camp	14/09/1918	16/09/1918
Miscellaneous			
War Diary	Winnezeele	17/09/1918	19/09/1918
War Diary	Right Batt. Canal Sector	20/09/1918	21/09/1918
War Diary	Ouderdom	22/09/1918	22/09/1918
Miscellaneous			
War Diary	Ouderdom	23/09/1918	26/09/1918
War Diary	Canal Sector Right Sub Sector	27/09/1918	27/09/1918
Miscellaneous			
War Diary	Right Sub Sector Canal Sector	28/09/1918	29/09/1918
War Diary	Ouderdom	30/09/1918	30/09/1918
Miscellaneous			
Heading	October 1918 War Diary Of 14th Battalion Argyll & Sutherland Highlanders Vol. XXVIII		
Miscellaneous			
War Diary	Ouderdom	01/10/1918	01/10/1918
War Diary	Wytschaete	02/10/1918	02/10/1918
War Diary	Ypres	03/10/1918	06/10/1918
Miscellaneous			
War Diary	Zonnebeke	07/10/1918	11/10/1918
Miscellaneous			
War Diary	Zonnebeke	12/10/1918	13/10/1918
War Diary	Kemmel	14/10/1918	15/10/1918
Miscellaneous			
War Diary	Maicornet	16/10/1918	16/10/1918
War Diary	Le Blaton	17/10/1918	17/10/1918
Miscellaneous			
War Diary	Le Blaton	18/10/1918	18/10/1918
War Diary	Neuville-En Ferrain	19/10/1918	19/10/1918
War Diary	Herseaux	20/10/1918	20/10/1918
War Diary	Evregnies	21/10/1918	21/10/1918
Miscellaneous			
War Diary	Warcoing	22/10/1918	23/10/1918
War Diary	Dottignies	24/10/1918	24/10/1918
Miscellaneous			
War Diary	Dottignies	25/10/1918	27/10/1918
War Diary	Helchin	28/10/1918	29/10/1918
Miscellaneous			
War Diary	Helchin	30/10/1918	31/10/1918
Miscellaneous			
Heading	Cover For Documents. Nature of Enclosures. War Diary Of The 14th Bn. Argyll & Sutherland Highlanders for the month of November 1918		
Miscellaneous			
War Diary	Herseaux	01/11/1918	05/11/1918
Miscellaneous			
War Diary	Herseaux	05/11/1918	08/11/1918
War Diary	Evregnies	09/11/1918	09/11/1918
Miscellaneous			
War Diary	Evregnies	10/11/1918	14/11/1918
Miscellaneous			
War Diary	Herseaux	15/11/1918	17/11/1918
Miscellaneous			
War Diary	Herseaux	18/11/1918	22/11/1918
Miscellaneous			

War Diary Miscellaneous	Herseaux	23/11/1918	27/11/1918
War Diary Miscellaneous	Herseaux	28/11/1918	30/11/1918
Heading	Cover For Documents. Nature of Enclosures. War Diary of the 14th Battn Arg & Suth'd Highrs for the month of December 1918 Vol 31		
Miscellaneous War Diary	Herseaux	01/12/1918	06/12/1918
Miscellaneous War Diary	Herseaux	07/12/1918	11/12/1918
Miscellaneous War Diary	Herseaux	12/12/1918	18/12/1918
Miscellaneous War Diary	Herseaux	19/12/1918	27/12/1918
Miscellaneous War Diary	Herseaux	28/12/1918	31/12/1918
Miscellaneous Heading	Cover For Documents. Nature of Enclosures. War Diary of the 14th Battn Argyll & Sutherland Highlanders for the month of January 1919 Vol 32		
Miscellaneous War Diary	Herseaux	01/01/1919	05/01/1919
Miscellaneous War Diary	Herseaux	05/01/1919	09/01/1919
Miscellaneous War Diary	Herseaux	10/01/1919	16/01/1919
Miscellaneous War Diary	Herseaux	17/01/1919	22/01/1919
Miscellaneous War Diary	Herseaux	23/01/1919	26/01/1919
Miscellaneous War Diary	Herseaux	27/01/1919	31/01/1919
Miscellaneous Heading	Cover For Documents. Nature of Enclosures. War Diary of the 14th Argyll & Sutherland Highlanders for the month of Feb. 1919 Vol 33		
Miscellaneous War Diary	Herseaux	01/02/1919	06/02/1919
Miscellaneous War Diary		07/02/1919	14/02/1919
Miscellaneous War Diary		16/02/1919	25/02/1919
Miscellaneous War Diary		26/02/1919	28/02/1919
Miscellaneous Heading	Vol XXXIII War Diary of the 14th Argyll & Sutherland Highlanders for the month of March 1919		
Miscellaneous War Diary	Herseaux	01/03/1919	08/03/1919
Miscellaneous War Diary	Herseaux	09/03/1919	19/03/1919
Miscellaneous War Diary	Herseaux	20/03/1919	28/03/1919
Miscellaneous War Diary	Herseaux	29/03/1919	31/03/1919

Miscellaneous Heading	War Diary of the 14th Argyll & Sutherland Highlanders for the month of April 1919 Vol. XXXIV		
Miscellaneous War Diary	Herseaux	01/04/1919	08/04/1919
Miscellaneous War Diary	Herseaux	09/04/1919	15/04/1919
Miscellaneous War Diary	Herseaux	16/04/1919	22/04/1919
Miscellaneous War Diary	Herseaux	23/04/1919	30/04/1919
Miscellaneous Heading	War Diary of the 14th Bn. Arg & Suth. Highrs. for the month of May 1919 Vol XXXIV		
Miscellaneous War Diary	Herseaux Belgium	01/05/1919	08/05/1919
Miscellaneous War Diary	Herseaux	09/05/1919	17/05/1919
Miscellaneous War Diary	Herseaux	18/05/1919	28/05/1919
Miscellaneous War Diary	Herseaux	29/05/1919	31/05/1919
Miscellaneous Heading	War Diary of 14th Argyll & Sutherland Highlanders for month of June 1919 Vol XXXVI		
Miscellaneous War Diary	Herseaux	01/06/1919	06/06/1919
Miscellaneous Heading	14th Division 42nd Infy Bde 9th Bn K.R.R.C. May 1915-Jun 1918 Disbanded 3.8.18		
Miscellaneous			

WO95 1900/1

14 DIV
42 Infantry Brigade
1918 APR - 1919 Jan

14th Battalion Argyll &
Sutherland Highlanders

14TH DIVISION
42ND INFY BDE

14TH BN A & S H.
~~APL~~ 1918-JUN 1919

From 40 DIV
 120 BDE

SECRET.   VOLUME XXIII.

WAR DIARY

OF THE

14th. BATTN. ARGYLL & SUTHERLAND HIGHLANDERS

FOR THE MONTH OF

APRIL - 1918.

IN THE FIELD.   COMMANDING 14th. Bn. A. & S.H.
5th. May, 1918.

14th S/qn A & S Highlanders.
WAR DIARY
VOLUME XXIII

Army Form C. 2118
APRIL 1918

INTELLIGENCE SUMMARY.
(Erase heading not required.)

Place	Date	Hour	Summary of Events and Information	Remarks and references to Appendices
FLEURBAIX RIGHT SUB-SECTOR	1/4/18		Weather fine. At 4.30 am hostile artillery opened out and shelled the Potez gun front on our unsupp sector. At 4.50 am our infantry companies were shelled. All quiet at 5.30 am. Casualties 1 killed and 1 wounded (O.R.) in A Company. Situation quiet for remainder of the day.	
- do -	2/4/18		Weather fine. Situation quiet. Slight hostile artillery activity during the day.	
- do -	3/4/18		Weather dull. Hostile artillery more active. 300 rounds 77 mm fired on HORNET'S NEST. Captain Kettle reported from Senior Officers School U.K.	
- do -	4/4/18		Weather dull. An unusual amount of transport & heard behind enemy lines during the night and evening. Our artillery fired 125 rounds on reported transport routes and traffic centres. Hostile artillery active during ten afternoon and evening. 14 - A & S H were relieved by 10/11th H.L.I. and withdrew to Reserve Battalion Reserve Brigade at SAILLY 2/7th Rls ld. 11/5 [illegible] from Reporters	

Army Form C. 2118

14th A & S Highlanders

WAR DIARY
INTELLIGENCE SUMMARY
Volume XXIII

APRIL 5/18

Instructions regarding War Diaries and Intelligence Summaries are contained in F.S. Regs., Part II. and the Staff Manual respectively. Title pages will be prepared in manuscript.

Place	Date	Hour	Summary of Events and Information	Remarks and references to Appendices
SAILLY	5/4/18		Weather dull. Battalion engaged in cleaning up. A draft of 220 O/R arrived at the Battalion	
-do-	6/4/18		Weather dull and showery. 2nd in command and 10 Officers per company reconnoitred Reserve position behind Portuguese at LAVENTIE	
-do-	7/4/18		Weather fair. The Battalion was broken up as follows :- 13 Officers and 276 O.R. left at 10 am to report to O.C. 1/7 A+S.H. 11 Officers and 220 O.R. left at 11 am to report to Rear Transport Depot 15th Division. H.Q. Company 6 Officers and 216 O.R. left at 3.15 pm for 30th Division & arrived and took over accommodation at "P" Camp POPERINGHE area. The Adjutant, Padre and M.O. remained with 40th Division.	
"P" Camp POPERINGHE AREA	8/4/18		Weather fair. H.Q. details engaged in cleaning up camp	
-do-	9/4/18		Weather dull. H.Q. details proceeded at 9.30 am and marched to ELVERDINGHE and troops over accommodation at WHITE MILL CAMP. 73 R.Sy. Aine attached to 1/4 A+S.H. Major C.C.y. Johnston proceeded to England.	

Army Form C.2118
14ᵗʰ /S/13 A⁷ᵗʰ S Atlantics

WAR DIARY
INTELLIGENCE SUMMARY. Volume XXIII

APRIL, 1918

(Erase heading not required.)

Instructions regarding War Diaries and Intelligence Summaries are contained in F.S. Regs., Part II. and the Staff Manual respectively. Title pages will be prepared in manuscript.

Place	Date	Hour	Summary of Events and Information	Remarks and references to Appendices
ELVERDINGHE	10/4/18		Weather fine. Major Kiddie and 2/Lt J Knowe reconnoitred "E" area. Batt. d up in camp with platoon.	
-do-	11/4/18		Weather fine. 2/Lt Simon returned from leave. Major Johnston and Capt. Wilson marched 36ᵗʰ in per area.	
-do-	12/4/18		Weather fine. Working party of 30 men under Major Coram proceeded to Reten up no god from Camp, formed firewoon on overurun 9/14ᵗʰ ATS. M leaving 40 Drawn Relieved by C.O.	
-do-	13/4/18		Weather fine. Working party of 80 men under Major poeta proceeded to	
-do-	14/4/18		Weather dull and windy. Working party of 80 men under Major proceeded to Major Johnstone. Major Kidder and Capt Wilson reconnoitred Corps line.	
-do-	15/4/18		Weather dull and windy. Working party of 30 men under Major proceeded Runner 90 Pcle. at MORDACQ FARM. Major Johnston and two platoon Relieved S R 36 ATS. M reconnoitred two new lines WEST of CHEEPSIDE.	
-do-	16/4/18		Weather dull. Party made Major Kaper relieved WHITE MILL CAMP Offer relieved by Belgians to 22 Corps area for the dumoon from New York with 100 O.R. himself by him	
BRANDHOEK	18/4/18		Weather dull and showery. Remainder of N.3 Coi. marched to ERIE CAMP BRANDHOEK Major J. Markowen of Johnson in other relief party.	
-do-	19/4/18		Weather dull. OC commander men working on BUSSYBOOM trenches	
BUYSSCHEURE	20/4/18		Weather dull. H.Q. moved by bus to BUYSSCHEURE and nearbilly. There.
	21/4/18		On leave from Hunters XB report. Major J Markowen took over command
	30/4/18			

A5834. Wt.W4973/M687 750,000 8/16 D.D. & L. Ltd. Forms/C.2118/13.

SECRET.

WAR DIARY

OF THE

14th. ARGYLL & SUTHERLAND HIGHLANDERS

FOR THE MONTH OF

M A Y - 1 9 1 8.

(VOLUME XXIV)

IN THE FIELD
5-6-18.

LIEUT. COLONEL,
COMMANDING 14th. ARGYLL & SUTHERLAND
HIGHLANDERS.

Army Form C. 2118.

WAR DIARY
14th Bn Arg. & Suth'd Highlanders
INTELLIGENCE SUMMARY.

MAY 1918.

VOL XXIV

(Erase heading not required.)

Instructions regarding War Diaries and Intelligence Summaries are contained in F. S. Regs., Part II. and the Staff Manual respectively. Title pages will be prepared in manuscript.

Place	Date	Hour	Summary of Events and Information	Remarks and references to Appendices
BUYSSCHEURE	1/5/18		Weather fine. Major C.L.G. Johnstone and Captain C.R.M. Miller took charge of a digging party of 65 other ranks composed of men of the Battalion and proceeded to WATTAU for attachment to 200 Company Royal Engineers	
do	2/5/18		Weather fine. Nothing of importance occurred.	
do	3/5/18		2nd Lieut W.L. Simson granted authority to wear badges of Captain while acting Adjutant from 22/4/18. 2nd Lieut A.R. Moffat appeared in DROs as having received "Italian Silver Medal" "for Valour".	
do	4/5/18		Weather showery. Nothing of importance occurred.	
do	5/5/18		Notifications of 12 other ranks receiving Military Medals in the operations near MORY, received.	NOMINAL ROLL SEE APPENDIX.
do	6/5/18		Captain W.S. Kilgour rejoined the Battalion from 8th Bn	
do	7/5/18		The Baths at BUYSSCHEURE were allotted to the Battalion today. Three O.R. rejoined the Battalion from 120th Light Mortar Battery	
do	8/5/18		Nothing of importance occurred	
do	9/5/18		Captain G.O.C. Smith M.C. rejoined the Battalion after tour of duty in U.K. Captain A.A. Chisholm rejoined the Battalion from 7th Bat	

WAR DIARY

14th Bn Bug of Suth Lys

INTELLIGENCE SUMMARY.

(Erase heading not required.)

MAY 1918   VOL. XXIV

Place	Date	Hour	Summary of Events and Information	Remarks and references to Appendices
BUYSSCHEURE	10/5/18		Nothing of importance occurred.	
do	11/5/18		Major I Mackinnon granted authority to wear badges of Lieut Col whilst commanding the Battalion. Officers under field rank vacated their Billets and moved into tents owing to shortage of accommodation for incoming troops.	
do	12/5/18		Orders as to disposal of transport received also surplus personnel.	
do	13/5/18		Transport left the Battalion for Base. Mess cart and Water cart retained also 7 Riders kept for Officers' use. Captain W.G.Y. Kiddie & Captain C.W.H. Fuller with 5 O.R. proceed to Gas Course.	
do	14/5/18		Captain G.A.C. Smith proceeded to hospital. The surplus to training establishment (150 O.R.) left Battalion marched to WATTEN where they entrained for ETAPLES.	
do	15/5/18		Training Staff left BUYSSCHEURE and marched to AUDRICQ where they entrained for WOINCOURT. Captain G.A.C. Smith rejoined the Battalion from hospital at AUDRICQ. Train left at 7.30 pm night spent in train.	
WOINCOURT	16/5/18		Detrained at WOINCOURT and marched to Billets in GAMACHES. Band left Battalion at Railhead and proceeded to Division for duty there	

Army Form C. 2118

WAR DIARY
4th Bn. Arg. & Suth'd Highlanders
INTELLIGENCE SUMMARY.
(Erase heading not required.) VOL XXIV

MAY 1918

Place	Date	Hour	Summary of Events and Information	Remarks and references to Appendices
GAMACHES	17/5/18		Received orders to join 31st American Infantry Battalion at LA HAIE Camp South of GAMACHES	
LA HAIE	18/5/18		Training commenced. Capt W.E.Y. Keddie MC and Capt C.W.H. Miller with 7 O.R. rejoined the Battalion from Corps Gas School	
do	19/5/18		No 9022 A/Cpl W.A. Buchanan received Bar to Military Medal while serving with 120th L.M.G. Battery. No 9201 Cpl J. Arton received Military Medal with 120 L.M.G. Batty.	
do	20/5/18		Demonstration Platoon from H.A.C. arrived.	
do	21/5/18		Training of Americans continued. American demonstration platoon arrived.	
do	22/5/18		Nothing of importance. Training continued.	
do	23/5/18		Nothing of importance. Training continued.	
do	24/5/18		Major O.C.G. Whistlers and Captain S.B.K. Corput, proceeded to base as being surplus to Cadre Establishment. Band rejoined the Battalion from playing American troops from Station to Staging Camp. Arrived. S/Sgt J. Howe reported to relieve S/Sgt J. Aelford who proceeded to UK for tour of duty. Captain S.B.K. Corput mentioned in Supplement to London Gazette.	

Army Form C. 2.

WAR DIARY
1/4 Arg Suther Highlanders
INTELLIGENCE SUMMARY.
VOL XXIV

MAY 1918

(Erase heading not required.)

Place	Date	Hour	Summary of Events and Information	Remarks and references to Appendices
LA HAIE	25/5/18		French Authorities ask for services of Band. Band proceeded to LE TREPORT and returned same night.	
do	26/5/18		Warning orders for move received.	
MILLE BOSC	27/5/18		Move to MILLE BOSC with detachment under Captain WGY Meddie MC with Captain CW Miller supplemented by 14 OR from 6th Bn. Wells Regiment at MONCHY to instruct 1st and 2nd Battalions 139 American Infantry respectively. Captain WSW Kilgore and Lieut A O Chisholm with 3 or respected the Battalion from Corps Gas School	
do	28/5/18		Training of 139th American Infantry commenced	
do	29/5/18		Captain R Dicks MC attached to 30th Division and taken on Strength of Batt.	
do	30/5/18		Holiday for American Troops. Sports arranged.	
do	31/5/18		Training continued. Route march by 1/139 Loyd Battalion.	

Geo Grant Lt Col
Comdg 14th Batte Bn Arg & Suth

WAR DIARY or INTELLIGENCE SUMMARY

Army Form C. 2118.

APPENDIX

The following nominal roll is extracted from 40th DRO 1949 of 3rd May 1918.

MILITARY MEDALS

No. 40591	Cpl	R. Hudson
9368	L/Cpl	P. Brogan
13529	Pte	C.W. Leask
12562	A/6.	F. Hutton
9649	Pte	T. McFarlane
9050	Cpl	P.J. Easdale
132555	Pte	A. Barclay
3725	"	P. McEwan
9248	"	E. Graham
300307	L/C	F. Holborow
300819	Pte	W. Ellies
12685	"	R.G. James

R. MacGrigor
Colonel
Commanding 102nd Bde. S. Inf.

128

90th Brigade.
30th Division.

Battalion transferred to 14th Division 15.5.18

CONFIDENTIAL

WAR DIARY

OF

14th Argt + Suth'd Highrs

FROM 1-6-18 TO 30-7-18

VOLUME NO. 25

Army Form C. 2118.

WAR DIARY VOLUME XXV
or
INTELLIGENCE SUMMARY

(Erase heading not required.)

-7 Jun 1918

14th Argyll & Sutherland Highlanders

Place	Date	Hour	Summary of Events and Information	Remarks and references to Appendices
MILLE BOSC	1/6/18		Weather fine. Training carried out in accordance with scheme.	WK
do.	2/6/18		Weather finer. Batt'n attended Divine Service.	WK
do.	3/6/18		Weather fine. Training carried out in accordance with scheme.	WK
do.	4/6/18		do.	WK
do.	5/6/18		Weather fine. 11.30 — Lewis Gun Coy. worked one hour's marching formation.	
do.	6/6/18		Weather fine. 11.30 — American supply train fit for landowners. Battn. in kind in. The Band played for the detachment. Advance party under Maj. E Bone and gave an Offr. and Others West & Advance party of Americans Battn. arrived o'pers. Spent the night in Billy Barencouchie.	WK

A.5384 Wt.W.4973/M687 750,000 8/16 D.D.&L. Ltd. Forms/C.2118/13.

VOLUME XXV
Army Form C. 2118.

WAR DIARY
or
INTELLIGENCE SUMMARY.

(Erase heading not required.)

June 1918

14th Argyll & Sutherland Highlanders

Place	Date	Hour	Summary of Events and Information	Remarks and references to Appendices
MILLE BOSC	7/6/18		American Bath. left Mille Bose. 2/Lt. M.H. Hill recommended for actual rank of Capt. from 22/4/18 — 8/5/18.	WK.
do.	8/6/18		Weather fine. Bath. attended Divine Service	WK.
do.	9/6/18		Weather fine. 2/Lt. Wilmot rejoined Battn. from hospital. Advance party American Battn. arrived.	WK.
do.	10/6/18		1 and 2/3rd American Coys. arrived	WK.
do.	11/6/18		Training carried out in accordance with scheme issued	WK.
do.	12/6/18 to 14/6/18		Weather fine. Training carried out. American Battn. trained forward w.W.K.	WK
do.	15/6/18		Weather fine. Left GAMACHES by train for ETAPLES.	WK.

A 5834 Wt. W4973/M687 750,000 8/16 D.D.& L. Ltd. Forms/C.2118/13.

VOLUME XXV
Army Form C. 2118.

June 1919

WAR DIARY
or
INTELLIGENCE SUMMARY.

(Erase heading not required.)

14th Argyll & Sutherland Highlanders.

Place	Date	Hour	Summary of Events and Information	Remarks and references to Appendices
ETAPLES	10/6/19		Arrived ETAPLES. Entrained for BOULOGNE. Billeted for night in OSTROHOVE Camp.	
BOULOGNE	11/6/19		Batt. marched from OSTROHOVE Camp to Quay. Embarked for U.K. Arrived at FOLKESTONE about 3 pm & entrained for BROOKWOOD, and proceeded to COWSHOT Camp. W.K.	

SECRET   VOLUME XXVI

WAR DIARY 42/14

OF THE

14th Argyll & Sutherland Highlanders.

FOR THE MONTH OF JULY

1918

[signature]
Lt. Col
Commdg 14th Batt. Arg & Suth'd. Hrs.

31st July. 1918.

June '19

WAR DIARY

OF THE

FOR THE MONTH OF JULY

1918

VOLUME XXVI

SECRET

Army Form C. 2118.

WAR DIARY
or
INTELLIGENCE SUMMARY.

14th Argyll & Sutherland Highlanders.   July 1918

(Erase heading not required.)

Place	Date	Hour	Summary of Events and Information	Remarks and references to Appendices
HAVRE	3/7/18		Battalion embarked at SOUTHAMPTON on 2/7/918 and disembarked at HAVRE on the 3/7/18	
BOULOGNE	4/7/18		Battalion embarked at FOLKESTONE on the "Golden Eagle" and disembarked at BOULOGNE at 12.10hrs.	
			The following Officers disembarked with the Battalion :-	
			Lt. Col. Mackinnon J	
			Capt. Kidd W.G.L. M.C. 2Lt. McShane W.A.J.	
			" Miller J.W.A. " Jamieson A.D.	
			" Smith Rae M.C. " Gemmell J	
			" Matthews J.H.O. M.C. " Grant L.B.	
			" Klapp M.D. " Am	
			" Mackenzie R.S. " Anderson O.F.	
			" Rodger C.H. " Macdougall A.H.	
			Lt. Thomson L.H.S. " Laing G.	
			" Crawford J.C. " Stewart E.	
			" Rankine J.C. " Naughton Lamont B.I	
			" Jacks A.C. " Davis Ross	
			" Mackie E.J.	
			" Kerr J.C.	
			" Angus A.M.	
			" Nobh Q.S.R.	
			Lieut W.J.	

136

Army Form C. 2118.

WAR DIARY
or
INTELLIGENCE SUMMARY.
(Erase heading not required.)

14th Argyll & Sutherland Highlanders.

July 1918

Place	Date	Hour	Summary of Events and Information	Remarks and references to Appendices
BOULOGNE	3/7/18		Maj. 3 Officers and 341 O.R.	
			T.Y. Woodhams will await 2nd Draft A.O.S. Argyle.	
			Batn. marched from Quay to L. Camp OSTROHOVE CAMP	W.E.
BOULOGNE	5/7/18		Battalion marched to BELLE to have transport returned	W.E.
BELLE	6/7/18		Weather fine	
			O.Rs. and Specialists moved out training from 9 am til 12 pm	
			Capt. R. Mackie C.F. reported to Batt. as Chaplain	W.E.
BELLE	7/7/18		Weather fine	
			Bath parade in Divine Service at 11:30 am	W.E.
BELLE	8/7/18		Weather fine	
			Coy specialist training carried out	
			Lt. Mathers (U.S. Army) reported to Batt. as M.O.	
			2/Lieut. Ridmills to hospital (sick)	W.E.
BELLE	9/7/18		Weather fine	
			Coy specialist training carried out	W.E.

Army Form C. 2118.

WAR DIARY
or
INTELLIGENCE SUMMARY.
(Erase heading not required.)

14th Argyll & Sutherland Highlanders.

July 1918

Instructions regarding War Diaries and Intelligence Summaries are contained in F. S. Regs., Part II. and the Staff Manual respectively. Title pages will be prepared in manuscript.

Place	Date	Hour	Summary of Events and Information	Remarks and references to Appendices
BELLE	10/7/18		Weather fair with heavy showers. Day specialist training carried out. Band informed that from base depot Sergt. E.S. Anderson reported to T.M.B.	WK
BELLE	11/7/18		Weather fine. Batt paraded at 9 a.m. and marched to BOURSIN in the following order - Band, "A" Coy, "B" Coy, "C" Coy, "D" Coy, Transport.	WK
BOURSIN	12/7/18		Weather Showery. Batt marched at 9.30 a.m. in the following order. Band, "A" Coy, "B" Coy, "C" Coy, "D" Coy, "A" Coy Transport, and marched to HOCQUINGHEM.	WK
HOCQUINGHEM	13/7/18		Weather fair. Batt paraded at 9.45 a.m. in the following order. Band, "A" Coy, "B" Coy, "C" Coy, "D" Coy, Transport and marched to LOUCHES.	WK
LOUCHES	14/7/18		Weather Showery. Specialists carried out one hours training. Lieut. Proceeded to 2nd Army School for 10 days course. 2/Lieut. Lang reported to Div. L.G. Coy to assist instructor.	WK

Army Form C. 2118.

WAR DIARY
or
INTELLIGENCE SUMMARY.
(Erase heading not required.)

14th Argyll & Sutherland Highlanders.

F ~ July 1918

Instructions regarding War Diaries and Intelligence Summaries are contained in F.S. Regs., Part II and the Staff Manual respectively. Title pages will be prepared in manuscript.

Place	Date	Hour	Summary of Events and Information	Remarks and references to Appendices
LOUCHES.	15/7/18		Weather fair but dull. Coy & Specialist training carried out. Masks during the day. Coy & Specialist training carried out. Batt. handed over and marched independently by Coys to NORDAUSQUE at time afforded. Waist Albdown.	WK
NORDAUSQUES	16/7/18		Weather fine but heavy thunderstorm in early morning. Coy & Specialist training carried out in the morning. Batt. paraded at 2pm for a rehearsal of Army Commanders Inspection tomorrow.	WK
NORDAUSQUES	17/7/18		Weather showery. Coy and Specialist training carried out in the forenoon. General Sewens inspected the Batt. at 2.30pm.	WK
NORDAUSQUES	18/7/18		Weather fair. Coy & Specialist training carried out from 9am - 12 noon and 2pm to 3pm.	WK
Nordausques	19/7/18		Weather fair. Coy & Specialist training carried out during the day.	WK

Army Form C. 2118.

WAR DIARY
or
INTELLIGENCE SUMMARY.
(Erase heading not required.)

14th Argyll & Sutherland Highlanders.

July 1918

Place	Date	Hour	Summary of Events and Information	Remarks and references to Appendices
Hargaousous	20/4/18		Walter shown on the Officers out rowing. Coy Special training in the forenoon. Educational training in the afternoon.	L/Cl
Do	21/4/18		Units at Sports. Bath Parade at 10 am to Douro Service. Draft of 20 O.R. joined the Batln. 41 O.R. proceeded to the base award list	
Do	22/4/18		Sunday Cov. Coy Specialist training. Coys & Companies and during the day. Adv't concert given in the evening.	
Do	23/4/18		Battalion Coy. Specialist training. Coys out during the day. 20 Officers joined the Batln.	L.K
Do	24/4/18		Weather cool. Coy Specialist training carried out. Batln. Proceeded to Monnecove by Cop & Baths. Sand traps (foot knives) to be sent away to 94th Field MC. extract from Reyts. All off. lof. Lieutr to be stamp Baptism	

Army Form C. 2118.

WAR DIARY
or
INTELLIGENCE SUMMARY.
(Erase heading not required.)

14th Argyll & Sutherland Highlanders.

Instructions regarding War Diaries and Intelligence Summaries are contained in F.S. Regs., Part II. and the Staff Manual respectively. Title pages will be prepared in manuscript.

Place	Date	Hour	Summary of Events and Information	Remarks and references to Appendices
Norgauques	21/7/18		Batt. Capt. taken to Granile permission to invest troops of rest of Brigade @ O.C. Churches @ Boiswell @ Boiswell Evening approval of G.O.C.	at Batt H.Q. Camp
Do	23/7/18		Weather fine Bn. Specialist Course carried out during the day	
Do	24/7/18		Weather stormy full use of dry C.S.M. & Coy Specialist training carried out	
Do	27/7/18		Weather rather wet Draft arrived with sun Scotch having arrived from an Army School 3 junior officers from our Battn. Draft of 30 O.R. under 2/Lt Watson joined Battn.	And
Do	28/7/18		Sunday Weather dull but dry Drew Parade at 10am for Divine Service Inter Company Knockout at football in the afternoon	...

Army Form C. 2118.

WAR DIARY
or
INTELLIGENCE SUMMARY.
(Erase heading not required.)

14th Argyll & Sutherland Highlanders.

July 1918

Instructions regarding War Diaries and Intelligence Summaries are contained in F. S. Regs., Part II. and the Staff Manual respectively. Title pages will be prepared in manuscript.

Place	Date	Hour	Summary of Events and Information	Remarks and references to Appendices
MORINGHEM	29/7/18		Battalion paraded at 10 a.m. in the following order: advance guard, Batln. Coy. HQ, A Coy, the Coy LMG, B Coy, HQ Coy Transport and marched to LE MARAIS. Battn. Horsewater park box & Command of Brigade School WK.	
LE MARAIS	30/7/18		Nothing fine. Battn. paraded at 10 a.m. in the following order: A Coy, B Coy, Coy of LMG, HQ & HQ Coy & Coy Transport and marched to NORDPEENE.	
NORDPEENE	31/7/18		Weather fine. Battn. paraded at 10.30 a.m. in the following order: advance guard, A Coy, B Coy, Coy of LMG, LMG Coy, HQ Coy, HQ Coy Transport and marched to bivouac at P.7.d.22 (Sheet 27 SE)	

Vol 24

WAR DIARY

SECRET

14TH ARG & SUTH'D HIGHRS

From 1-8/8-18 To 31-8/8-18

Vol 27

Army Form C. 2118

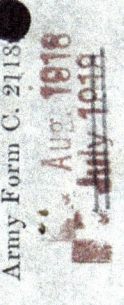
Aug 1918
July 1918

WAR DIARY
or
INTELLIGENCE SUMMARY
14th Argyll & Sutherland Highlanders.

(Erase heading not required.)

Place	Date	Hour	Summary of Events and Information	Remarks and references to Appendices
ST. SYLVESTRE CAPPEL	1/8/18		Weather showery. Working party of 100 O.R. on defensive system under R.E. Battalion stood to in battle positions in WINNIZEELE LINE.	W.K.
do.	2/8/18		Weather showery. Working party of 50 O.R. per day on defensive system under R.E. and specialist training in the forenoon. Sport in the afternoon.	W.K.
do.	3/8/18		Weather showery. Battalion engaged in work in the forenoon on defensive system. Specialist training in the forenoon. Recreational training in the afternoon. Capt. N.D. Chisholm proceeded on leave. 2/Lt Stephen took over command of "C"Coy.	W.K.
do.	4/8/18		Sunday. Weather dull. Battalion paraded at 10 a.m. for Divine Service. Sport in the afternoon. Draft of 19 O.R. arrived at Reinft.	W.K.

WAR DIARY
or
INTELLIGENCE SUMMARY

14th Argyll & Sutherland Highlanders

Army Form C. 2118

Aug. 1918

Place	Date	Hour	Summary of Events and Information	Remarks and references to Appendices
St SYLVESTRE CAPPEL	5/8/18		Weather dull showers. 6 Officers and 70 O.R. attended Divisional Horse Show at EPERLECQUES. Commanding Officer and Capt. G.A.C. Smith M.C. & Capt MacKenzie attended Conference at TER DEGHEM. A.& B. Coys at Baths. Remainder of Batt. worked on defensive lines under R.E. Lt Mackay proceeded to Infantry Course VII Corps School Lt C.A. Tulloh proceeded to Bombing Course VII Corps School 2Lt Stewart proceeded to L.G. Course VII Corps School.	W.M. W.M.
do.	6/8/18		Weather dull. Lewis gunners & Signallers on Specialist training. Remainder of Batt. working on defensive system.	W.M.
do.	7/8/18		Weather fair. Lewis gunners & signallers on specialist training. Remainder of Batt. worked on defensive system. Recreational training in the afternoon.	W.M.

Army Form C. 2118

WAR DIARY
or
INTELLIGENCE SUMMARY.

14th Argyll & Sutherland Highlanders

July 1918
Aug. 1918

(Erase heading not required.)

Instructions regarding War Diaries and Intelligence Summaries are contained in F. S. Regs., Part II. and the Staff Manual respectively. Title pages will be prepared in manuscript.

Place	Date	Hour	Summary of Events and Information	Remarks and references to Appendices
ST. SYLVESTRE CAPPEL	1/8/18		Weather fair. Lewis Gunners & Signallers under specialist officers. Remainder of Batt. march in offensive lines. No 4 Platoon under 2/Lt Jacks proceeded on attachment (Command Brigade) Plat. H.Qr. BAYENGHOVE. Draft of 23 O.R. under Lt G.S. Hillier joined the Batt.	W.D.
do.	2/8/18		Weather fair. Lewis Gunners & Signallers on specialist training. Remainder of Batt. on work in forenoon. Recreational training in afternoon.	W.D.
do.	3/8/18		Weather fine. Lewis Gunners & Signallers on specialist training. Remainder of Batt. work in the forenoon. Recreational training in afternoon.	W.D.

Army Form C. 2118

WAR DIARY
or
INTELLIGENCE SUMMARY
(Erase heading not required)

14th Argyll & Sutherland Highlanders

July 1918 Aug. 1918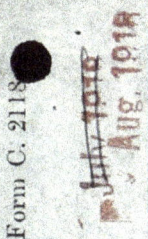

Instructions regarding War Diaries and Intelligence Summaries are contained in F. S. Regs., Part II. and the Staff Manual respectively. Title pages will be prepared in manuscript.

Place	Date	Hour	Summary of Events and Information	Remarks and references to Appendices
ST SYLVESTRE CAPPEL	11/8/18		Weather fine. Sunday. Coys Grenades & Lewis Gunners carried out scheduled training & remainder of Batt. on Inspn in the forenoon. Batt. Sports in the afternoon.	W.L.
do.	12/8/18		Weather fine. Batt marched off in two parties: 1st at 8 am, 2nd at 10.45 am to STEENVOORDE Station and proceeded thence by rail to ST MOMELIN, where they detrained & marched to ZUDROVE.	W.L.
ZUDROVE	13/8/18		Weather fine. Batt moved off at 10 am & marched to BAYENGHEM-LEZ-EPERLECQUES.	W.L.
BAYENGHEM	14/8/18		Weather fine. Coys & specialists carried out fresh hours training in the morning. Sport in the afternoon.	W.L.

Army Form C. 2118

July 1918
& Aug. 1918

WAR DIARY
or
INTELLIGENCE SUMMARY
(Erase heading not required.)

14th Argyll & Sutherland Highlanders

Instructions regarding War Diaries and Intelligence Summaries are contained in F.S. Regs., Part II. and the Staff Manual respectively. Title pages will be prepared in manuscript.

Place	Date	Hour	Summary of Events and Information	Remarks and references to Appendices
BAYENGHEM	15/8/18		Weather fine. Coy's & specialists carried out 4 hours training in the forenoon. Sports in the afternoon.	W.S.
do.	16/8/18		Weather fine. Coy's & specialists carried out 2½ hours training. Bath at Baths at EPERLECQUES.	W.S.
do.	17/8/18		Weather fine. Coy's & specialists carried out 4 hours training in the forenoon. Recreational training in the afternoon.	W.S.
do.	18/8/18		Sunday. Weather fine. Batt. paraded at 10 a.m. for Divine Service. 2 Lt. Noble reported from Canadian.	W.S.
do.	19/8/18		Weather fine. Batt. paraded at 9.4.5 a.m. marched to LOUCHES. Lt. Chisholm reported at 2 Brigade H.Q. as Intelligence Officer.	W.S.

Army Form C. 2118

WAR DIARY
or
INTELLIGENCE SUMMARY.
(Erase heading not required.)

14th Argyll & Sutherland Highlanders.

July 1918
Aug 1918

Place	Date	Hour	Summary of Events and Information	Remarks and references to Appendices
LOUCHES	30/7/18		Weather fine. Lt-Col Mackinnon took over command part 2 Inf. Brigade. Major Eadie M.C. took over command of Batt. Major Mills took over duties of 2/c in command of Batt. 2/Lt Crawford took over command of "A" Coy. Capt Chisholm returned from leave, took over command W.O.'s.	W.R.
do.	31/7/18		Batt. on range at GUEMY. Recreational training in afternoon. Weather splendid. Coys carried out training in the forenoon. Batt played 62 Field Coy. R.E. at football in afternoon.	W.R.
do.	1/8/18		Weather fine. Batt. on range at GUEMY. Recreational training in afternoon. Lt Shepshire transferred from "C" Coy to "A" Coy.	W.R.

Army Form C. 2118

WAR DIARY
or
INTELLIGENCE SUMMARY. 14th Argyll & Sutherland Highlanders

(Erase heading not required.)

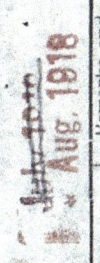
Aug. 1918

Place	Date	Hour	Summary of Events and Information	Remarks and references to Appendices
LOUCHES.	23/8/18		Weather fine. Batt. paraded at 6 a.m. marched to military siding at NORTKERQUE where Other Ranks entrained for PROVEN. Detrained at PROVEN and marched to TUNNELLING Camp.	N.W.
PROVEN	24/8/18		Weather fair. Batt engaged in cleaning up Camp. Inspection parade held by O.C. Recreational training in afternoon. C.O. to Chicken hut re: convenient Brigade scheme. Mee Capt. Horsncel (?) 2 Lt Hepburn proceed to 14 Army School. Draft 1 Lt. S.A. reported to Batt. Lt Clark and 2 Lt Milne D.C. reported to Batt.	
	25/8/18		Weather fair. Batt paraded for Divine Service at 10 a.m. Batt played WILTS at football in headquarters. Beth/4 Wilts 1/-	

Army Form C. 2118

WAR DIARY
or
INTELLIGENCE SUMMARY.
(Erase heading not required.)

14th Argyll & Sutherland Highlanders.

Aug. 1918

Place	Date	Hour	Summary of Events and Information	Remarks and references to Appendices
PROVEN	28/8/18		Capt. W.N. Kilgour returned to Batt from Course and took over command of "C" Coy. Capt Mackenzie proceeded to Kemmel Signal School. Lt Shepstone took over command of "B" Coy. 2nd Lts Jacks and M. 4 Platoon rejoined Batt. from detachment duty.	
do.	26/8/18		Weather wet. Batt engaged in work on defensive lines.	
do.	27/8/18		Weather dull. Batt engaged in work on defensive lines. 2nd Lts Andrus and 16 O.R. reported to 42 Brigade H.Q. for liaison duty. Lt C.A. Miller and 2 Lt Johnston returned from Course.	

Army Form C. 2118

WAR DIARY
or
INTELLIGENCE SUMMARY.

14th Argyll & Sutherland Highlanders
JULY 1918
Aug. 1918

(Erase heading not required.)

Instructions regarding War Diaries and Intelligence Summaries are contained in F. S. Regs., Part II. and the Staff Manual respectively. Title pages will be prepared in manuscript.

Place	Date	Hour	Summary of Events and Information	Remarks and references to Appendices
PROVEN	29/8/18		Weather dull & showery. Coy. at school of Coy. commanders for training from 9 a.m. to 12 noon.	
PROVEN	29/8/18		Weather fair. Batt. paraded at 1 p.m. entrained and proceeded by light railway to B.20.6.1.7. (sheet 28 N.W.) where they detrained and marched to SIEGE CAMP (B.27.a) and took over accommodation vacated by 16 Scottish Rifles.	WR.
SIEGE CAMP	30/8/18		Weather fair. Specialists & Coys carried out training from 9 a.m. to 12 noon. Sports in the afternoon.	WR.
do.	31/8/18		Weather fair. Coys and specialists training from 9 a.m. – 12 noon. Batt. at Baths at Siege Camp. S.O. reconnoitred front line of Left Batt. Left Brigade at YPRES.	WR.

152

CONFIDENTIAL

WAR DIARY

OF

14th Bn gt Suffolk Hghrs

FROM 1-9-18 TO 30-9-18

VOLUME
NO
28

Army Form C. 2118.

WAR DIARY
or
INTELLIGENCE SUMMARY.
(Erase heading not required)

14th Argyll & Sutherland Highlanders.

*- Sep. 1915.

Instructions regarding War Diaries and Intelligence Summaries are contained in F. S. Regs., Part II. and the Staff Manual respectively. Title pages will be prepared in manuscript.

Place	Date	Hour	Summary of Events and Information	Remarks and references to Appendices
SIEGE CAMP	1/9/15		Weather fair. Battalion paraded at 10 a.m. for Divine Service. Sports in the Afternoon. Lieut Strachan reported to Battalion from In Corp Schie. and S.O.R. reported to Battalion from In Corp Schie. 2/Lieut h. Weekes appointed O/c Section of Our Post train	
Do	2.9.15.		Weather fair. Companies and Specialists carried out training from 9am to 12 noon. Afloat in the Afternoon.	
Do	3/9/15		Weather fair. Companies carried out training from 9am to 12 noon. D.O. 2/Lt a Cameron Ro. and transport took quarter's premises front line of Reff Battalion 4th Brigade at II hooks in front of YPRES	
Do	4/9/15		Weather fair. Batt carried out training from 9.30am to 12 noon. Morning Parks of 1 Company and half hooking on defensive fire. 1 Officer 2 N.C.Os of R/H 4th 1 Off. N.C.o. 1 h.Co. 2.H. started proceeded to Armin Post to Reff Battalion through Left Out section 14th Division	

WAR DIARY
or
INTELLIGENCE SUMMARY.
(Erase heading not required.)

Army Form C. 2118.

Sep. 1918

14th Argyll & Sutherland Highlanders.

Place	Date	Hour	Summary of Events and Information	Remarks and references to Appendices
SIEGE CAMP	5/9/18		Weather fine. Battalion on Wilhelm Parade and cleaning up. Tank crew. Black reported that Lieut Regnart (also of Belgian Army) an baron officer had passed at 6:30 bu enroute to SPRA or B2B.17 (Lieut 25) and returned at OOSTERLA statu. Met A&SH relieved B' Coy Liaison Right D' Coy C' Bond A' ... Once relief of the Gas shelter fell across B' Coy 118a.	nil
Left Batt. Eqt-Sub Secto YPRES.	6/9/18		For Wilson from will kick ground most in morning to be shortened took one hour made from asparagus Situation - normal.	nil
Do.	7/9/18		Patrol under 2/Lieut J.B. Ignatus took 7 prisoners of the 27 Bav. Regiment Lieut O'Callaghan/Mathis have return in the Evening 2 Lieut Q.A. J Balcony wounded 2 killed, 2 wounded and 1 missing Capt A.M. Coupar proceeded to IX Corps Intelligence School	nil
Do.	8/9/18		Weather fair. Situation Quiet. 1 N.C.O. wounded. Lieut J. Marshall joined the Battn.	nil

WAR DIARY or INTELLIGENCE SUMMARY

Army Form C. 2118.

Sep. 1918

14th Argyll & Sutherland Highlanders

Place	Date	Hour	Summary of Events and Information	Remarks and references to Appendices
Left RAIL Siding under YPRES	9/9/18		Weather fair. Situation quiet.	nil
Do	10/9/18		Weather fair with showers. Situation quiet.	nil
Do	11/9/18		Weather dull but showers. Situation quiet. Got no news reported from front.	nil
Do	12/9/18		Weather dull. Situation quiet.	nil
Do	13/9/18		Weather dull. Situation quiet. 8th Inniskillings the W. on the left front left and Berks on the right. 14th A & S Hrs. sent down to O Camp DIRTY BUCKET CAMP	nil
Dirty Bucket Camp	14/9/18		Weather case. Activity. Troops Australian. Moved on Leave.	nil
Do	15/9/18		Weather fair. Battalion paraded at 9.15am and marched to TRIANGLE where they entrained at KINEO.8 and took over accommodation in WINNEZEELE	nil
Do	16.9.18		Weather fine. Day specialists paraded out 4 hours training.	nil

WAR DIARY
or
INTELLIGENCE SUMMARY

Army Form C. 2118

1st Sep. 1917

14th Argyll & Sutherland Highlanders.

Place	Date	Hour	Summary of Events and Information	Remarks and references to Appendices
WINNEZEELE	17/9/16		Weather fine. Scouts carried out 4 hours training at Zaggelles. C.O. reconnoitred front line Canal Sector Right Battalion	mps
Ao.	18/9/16		Weather fine. Reinforcements carried out thoroughly training. Platoon & Coy in Attack. 1st Officer & 1 Officer per Coy, with 1st Sergeant and 1 N.C.O. per Platoon proceeded as advance party to Right Battalion in CANAL SECTOR	mps
Ao.	19/9/16		Weather fair. Scouts toowards inspected a Company Battalion entrained at 5pm. and detrained at PIONEER SIDING Battalion took over Right Front of CANAL SECTOR from 15th Cheshire Regt. "A"Coy. Left front, "C"Coy. RIGHT FRONT, "B"Coy Support, "D"Coy RESERVE. Quiet relief.	mps
RIGHT BATT. CANAL SECTOR	20/9/16		Weather fair. Situation quiet. Lt. A.P.R. Waterproceeded to UK to resign his commission & take up medical studies	mps
Ao.	21/9/18		Weather fair. Situation quiet. Divisional Commander visited the Sector. Bn. was relieved by 16th Manchester Regt & battalion to BILLETS at OUDERDOM. No. 2 Coy in BOND at Buckbrough under Major 10 Q.T. Kerrie M.C.	mps
OUDERDOM	22/9/16		Weather dull & showery. Parts resting, cleaning up and making up deficiencies. C.O. attended Conference	mps

WAR DIARY
or
INTELLIGENCE SUMMARY.

(Erase heading not required.)

14th Argyll & Sutherland Highlanders Sep. 1918

Army Form C. 2118

Place	Date	Hour	Summary of Events and Information	Remarks and references to Appendices
OUDERDOM	23/9/18		Weather fine. A & C Coys carried out training in the forenoon	mss
Do.	24/9/18		Weather showery. A & C Coys carried out training in the forenoon. 2Lt A.W. Angus reported for duty. B Coys to Intelligence School. 2Lt A. Gordon reported to Batt. and taken on the strength.	mss
Do.	25/9/18		Weather showery in morning, fair in the afternoon. A & C Coys carried out training.	mss
Do.	26/9/18		Weather fair. Rain making up afternoon. Lt A/Major relieved 16 Manchester Regt. in CANAL Sector. Right Coy Sector. A Coy in left front, C Coy on right front. B Coy in support in front of (called wood). D Coy in Reserve in Dickebusch Huts. Bn in Dickebusch Hunt. Quiet night.	mss
CANAL SECTOR Right Sub Sector	27/9/18		Weather fine. Battalion Headquarters and B Coy moved to VOORMEZEELE Sector.	mss

Army Form C. 2118

WAR DIARY
or
INTELLIGENCE SUMMARY.
(Erase heading not required.)

14th Argyll & Sutherland Highlanders.

Sep. 1918

Instructions regarding War Diaries and Intelligence Summaries are contained in F. S. Regs., Part II. and the Staff Manual respectively. Title pages will be prepared in manuscript.

Place	Date	Hour	Summary of Events and Information	Remarks and references to Appendices
RIGHT SUB SECTOR CANAL SECTOR	28/9/18	10am	Battalion took up position for the attack "A" at keep deploying in front of FRENCH TRENCH	
		5.30am	After our artillery & machine gun barrage of about 5 minutes, the Battalion launched the attack from ST ELOI CRATERS to PICCADILLY FARM	
		7am	Final objective taken. Casualties:- both R.& L. Smith M.C. & 3. O.R. killed. 43 wounded. War trophies:- 80. War trophies:- 6 machine guns & 4 trench mortars	MD
			Prisoners Captured:- 80.	MD
Do.	29/9/18		Bull with Lewis gun consolidate line of final objective. Established post beyond the DAMSTRASSE. Battalion withdraws to billets in OUDERDOM at 3pm. Balance went through process on leave.	MD
OUDERDOM	30/9/18		Parade. Bull went at every occupation. Spent day cleaning up. Capt R.a.G. Smith M.C. buried at 11am in OUDERDOM Cemetery.	MD

OCTOBER 1918

WAR DIARY

OF

14th Battalion Argyll & Sutherland Highlanders

Vol. XXVIII

J. Thackthwaite
Lieut-Col.
Comdg 14th Bn Arg & S Hrs

WAR DIARY or INTELLIGENCE SUMMARY

Army Form C. 2118.

Place	Date	Hour	Summary of Events and Information	Remarks and references to Appendices
OUDERDOM	1.10.18		Weather fair with some showers. Battalion moved off at 12.45 to WYTSCHAETE and arrived at 15.00	
WYTSCHAETE	2.10.18		Weather fair. Battalion left WYTSCHAETE at 11.00 and arrived at WULVERGHEM at 14.30 and entrained (for YPRES (HELLFIRE CORNER) at 19.00) arrived there at 02.30 (3-10-18) 2.M. Stewart admitted to hospital sick	
YPRES	3.10.18		Weather bad. Battalion engaged in making billets.	
do.	4.10.18		Weather fine. Battalion engaged in unloading railhead on road at CLAPHAM JUNCTN (Sheet 28 1/40000 J.13.b.5.0.)	
do.	5.10.18		Weather fair with showers. Battalion engaged in work on YPRES - ZONNEBEKE Rd. Capt Scott took party near railway, burial of 9th Division call N.L. SIMON proceeded on leave.	
do.	6.10.18		Weather rather dull. Battalion worked on YPRES-ZONNEBEKE Rd. 2.M. E.B. LOWNDES proceeded to Rest Camp, LE TOUQUET.	

WAR DIARY
or
INTELLIGENCE SUMMARY.
(Erase heading not required.)

Army Form C. 2118

Place	Date	Hour	Summary of Events and Information	Remarks and references to Appendices
ZONNEBEKE	7.10.18		Weather fair with some rain. Half Battalion working on road. Remained half night camp to ZONNEBEKE.	WX
do.	8.10.18		Weather inclement. Battalion working on road. Rations & gun stores carried. One man accidentally wounded by bayonet.	WX
do.	9.10.18		Weather improved. Battalion working on road. Lieut Commdr Clayed on transport. Lt. Col. MacKenzie proceeded on leave & Major Henderson took over command. Major C.B. MacKenzie took over duties of 2nd in Command.	WX
do.	10.10.18		Weather inclement. Battalion working on road. Reinforcement Camp was taken over. Lt. R.S. Willis reported from II Army school of Musketry. 1 M. wounded from shell-fire and was sent to C Coy.	WX
do.	11.10.18		Weather inclement. Battalion inspected overcoats & boots.	WX

WAR DIARY
or
INTELLIGENCE SUMMARY.

(Erase heading not required.)

Army Form C. 2118

Place	Date	Hour	Summary of Events and Information	Remarks and references to Appendices
ZONNEBEKE	12.10.18		Weather dull intermittent rain. Battalion engaged in work on road. 2 Lt Hepburn proceeded with 10 men to YPRES Camp AUDRESELLES.	W.R.
do	13.10.18		Weather dull: heavy mists & showers. Battalion moved at 06.30 and marched to HELLFIRE CORNER, entrained at 09.00 for PADDINGTON JUNCT: Arrived at 13.30. Proceeded & billeted in area N.31.a. (Sheet 28) on slopes of KEMMEL HILL.	W.R.
KEMMEL	14.10.18		Weather dull. Batt: ordered to be prepared to move at one hours notice in consequence of Cooks attack at 05.30. Germans withdrew in consequence. Hostile shellfire. 4 men wounded by shellfire.	W.R.
do.	15.10.18		Weather fair. Battalion moved at 07.00 to WULVERGHEM arriving at 10.20. Marched at 18.20 to relieve 33 London (R.B.) in the batt: N.W. Sector MAI CORNET (S. of COMINES). Relief complete at 03.30 on 16.10.18.	W.R.

WAR DIARY
or
INTELLIGENCE SUMMARY.

(Erase heading not required.)

Army Form C. 2118

Place	Date	Hour	Summary of Events and Information	Remarks and references to Appendices
HALLOCOURT	6.10.18		Weather cloudy with occasional showers. Patrols sent out at dawn towards STE MARGUERITE Church. No enemy. Bn. relieved at 14.00 hours in order A, D, B, C, Coys. Objective LE BLATON, LES DRIARDS. At 17.00 hours A Coy held up by M.G. fire on outskirts of LE BLATON. B Coy pushed out patrols to locate M.G. At 21.00 hours points obtained by 12th SUFFOLKS & 3 Bde. on left flank. At 22.00 hours reoccupied LE BLATON and linked up with 1/F E 4th & 31st Division on right flank. 2 L Crawford & 2 Lt Counsell relieved from Corps School. Lt Welbourn returned. Others on leave.	
LE BLATON	7.10.18		Weather fine. Battalion out on 1 hour at 10.0 hours by 4.3 hours and 31 Bns. and relieved with Billets at LE HALLOT. Battalion moved at 17.00 hours billets between LE BLATON and LINSELLES. Capt. McKergow reported from leave. Lt W. J. Walker proceeded on leave. Lt Walton succeeded will.	

By Commanders Orders

WAR DIARY
or
INTELLIGENCE SUMMARY.

(Erase heading not required.)

Army Form C. 2118

Instructions regarding War Diaries and Intelligence Summaries are contained in F. S. Regs., Part II. and the Staff Manual respectively. Title pages will be prepared in manuscript.

Place	Date	Hour	Summary of Events and Information	Remarks and references to Appendices
LE BIZET	18.10.18		Weather fine. Battalion moved from 13.30 hours to the old billets in NEUVILLE-EN-FERRAIN. Arrived at 15.45.	WK
NEUVILLE-EN-FERRAIN	19.10.18		Weather dull & misty. Battalion moved that 08.15 & marched to MONT-A-LEUX, arriving at 10.00; moved on again at 15.30 hours & arrived in HERSEAUX at 17.30.	WK
HERSEAUX	20.10.18		Weather dull & wet. Battalion marched at 09.00 and S arrived at EVREGNIES at 11.30 hours. Details joined Batt. at 16.00 hours.	
EVREGNIES	21.10.18		Weather dull & mild. Lt Mackay proceeded on leave. Lt Warhide to 31 Army School. Musketry. 2.lt. Thompson to Infantry Revolver School. Battalion moved that 17.00 hours & relieved 12 Suffolk Regt. in Rifle Batt front N of WARCOING. "C" Coy. left front. "D" Coy right. "A" Coy support. "B" Coy in reserve. WARCOING - Bn. Head. Shells. A little shelling around Bn. H. Q.	WK WK WK WK

WAR DIARY or INTELLIGENCE SUMMARY

Army Form C. 2118

Place	Date	Hour	Summary of Events and Information	Remarks and references to Appendices
WARCOING	22.10.18		Weather milder, showers. Hostile artillery fairly active during the day. Relieving "B" Coy. took over Coy. with Hqrs. F. left support. "A" Coy. remained in R.I. support. "D" Coy. withdrew to reserve. Quiet relief.	
do.	23.10.18		Weather fine but moist. Hostile artillery fairly active during the day. 6th Welsh Regt. relieved 15A & 5A who withdrew to Buissen. D. o. T. & G. N. I. E. S. Quiet relief. 2/Lt. ATHEY reported to Batt. 2/Lt Sexsmith reported from hospital. 2/Lt Crack reported to Batt.	OK
DOTTIGNIES	24.10.18		Weather fair. Batt. employed in bathing and cleaning up. 4 killed and 16 other casualties to Shellfire. Lt. Shelston proceeded to L.G. course at G.H.Q. 2/Lt Cox proceeded on leave. 2/Lt Launders M.C. reported from Rest Camp.	

Army Form C. 2118

WAR DIARY
or
INTELLIGENCE SUMMARY.
(Erase heading not required.)

Instructions regarding War Diaries and Intelligence Summaries are contained in F. S. Regs., Part II. and the Staff Manual respectively. Title pages will be prepared in manuscript.

Place	Date	Hour	Summary of Events and Information	Remarks and references to Appendices
DOTTIGNIES	25/10/18		Weather fine. Corps concentrated transport from O.F. 20 — 12.30.	bk.
do.	26/10/18		Weather fine. Corps arrived and transport from O.F. 20 — 12.30. 2 Lt Jamieson returned from Corps Res/Camp. G.O.C. Division visited Battalion.	bk
do.	27/10/18		Sunday. Weather fine. Service in the hutment. Capt. T.O. and one other for Coy reconnoitred the HELCHIN front. SECTOR. H.E.A.d.S.A. marched off at 17.00 hours to relieve 4th Cy K. Hamptons. Lt & QM 3 Corps 2 Lt LANCE w/ HELCHIN front & ESCAUT Line. Small relief.	ESCAUT bad
HELCHIN	28/10/18		Weather fine. Relief in quiet. 2 Lt Hepburn reported from 2 Army Rest Camp.	bk
do.	29/10/18		Weather fine. Hostile heavy artillery shelled our front line. G.O.C. Division visited Battalion. Lt Col. Hawkins M/C returned from leave.	bk

WAR DIARY
or
INTELLIGENCE SUMMARY.

Army Form C. 2118

Place	Date	Hour	Summary of Events and Information	Remarks and references to Appendices
HELCHIN	30/10/18		Weather fine. Situation quiet. 2/Lt LOWNDES took 3 runners of 3 Fwd Coy. M.M. (3 Pdrs.) on patrol.	
Do.	31/10/18		Weather still showery. Situation quiet. 14 W.H.O. were relieved by 33 London Regt. (A.B). Fresh relief. 14th Batt. marched to HERSEAUX to billets. A Divisional Routine Order 31st Oct. 1918. the following honours were awarded to O.R. of the Bar.	
			254301 F/Cpl W. MANDELKAN M.M. Bar to M.M.	
			15859 Pte J Gibson	M.M.
			254299 Pte H.C. BLEAKLEY	M.M.
			293508 Pte J STEWART	M.M.
			4103 Pte R. ROBERTSON	M.M.

SECRET

Army Form W.3091.

Cover for Documents.

Nature of Enclosures.

WAR DIARY

OF THE

14th Bn Argyll & Sutherland Highlanders.

FOR THE MONTH OF

NOVEMBER 1918

Lt. Col.
Comdg. 14th Bn. Arg & Suth'd. Hrs.

Notes, or Letters written.

Army Form C. 2118.

WAR DIARY
or
INTELLIGENCE SUMMARY.

(Erase heading not required.)

Place	Date	Hour	Summary of Events and Information	Remarks and references to Appendices
HERSEAUX	1/11/18		Weather fine. Bath engaged in cleaning up. Lt. M.H. Hill returned from leave. Lt. 6 O.R.s admitted to hospital.	W.K.
do.	2/11/18		Weather fine. Coys carried out 2½ hours training. Baths at HERSEAUX were allotted to Coys.	W.K.
do.	3/11/18		Sunday. Weather fine. Battalion paraded for Divine Service at 1000 hours. 2 Lt. Aitken admitted to hospital.	W.K.
do.	4/11/18		Weather fine. Coys carried out training from 0900 – 1100 hours & from 1400 to 1500 hours. 2 Lt. Jaikes proceeds to II Army Rest Camp PARIS PLAGE.	W.K.
do.	5/11/18		Weather rather dull. Coys carried out training in billets from 0900 – 1200 hours from 1400 – 1500 hours.	W.K.

WAR DIARY or INTELLIGENCE SUMMARY

Army Form C. 2118.

Nov. 1918

Place	Date	Hour	Summary of Events and Information	Remarks and references to Appendices
HERLEAUX	5/11/18		Lt. D.G. Shedden to be a/Capt. whilst Comdg. a Coy. (from 17.10.18) Lt. J.F. Madden to be a/Capt. whilst Comdg. a Coy. (from 13.10.18) Lt. Walker reported from leave.	W.R.
do.	6/11/18		Weather dull & showery. Coys carried out training from 0900 – 1200 hours & from 1400 – 1500 hours. Lt Findlay-Thompson & Lt Marshall reported from Composite Batt.	W.R.
do.	7/11/18		Weather dull & wet. Coys carried out training from 0900 – 1200 hours & from 1400 – 1500 hours.	W.R.
do.	8/11/18		Weather dull & showery. Coys carried out mechanics training. Batt. moved that 150 ohms and took over billets at EVREGNIES vacated by 12th Suffolk Regt.	W.R.
EVREGNIES	9/11/18		Weather fine. Coys carried out 4 hours training.	W.R.

Army Form C. 2118.

WAR DIARY
of
INTELLIGENCE SUMMARY.

(Erase heading not required.)

Instructions regarding War Diaries and Intelligence
Summaries are contained in F. S. Regs., Part II.
and the Staff Manual respectively. Title pages
will be prepared in manuscript.

Place	Date	Hour	Summary of Events and Information	Remarks and references to Appendices
EVREGNIES	10/11/18		Sunday, weather cold and fine. Batt. paraded for divine service at 1000 hours.	W.J.
do.	11/11/18		Weather dull. Batt. paraded at 0900 for ceremonial drill. Armistice came into force at 1100 hours.	W.J.
do.	12/11/18		Weather fine. Batt. carried out 4 hours training.	W.J.
do.	13/11/18		Weather fine. Coys carried out 1½ hours training. Batt. bathed parades at Baths at DOTTIGNIES. Lt. & Qmr. Weir proceeded on leave. 2 Lt Jackes reported from Rest Camp PARIS PLAGE.	W.J.
do.	14/11/18		Weather cold but fine. Batt. marched out 10.30 hours and took over billets at HERSEAUX. Reliefs by 33 London Regt.(R.B.) Caps. W.W. Kilpin, Capt. W.R. Lines, Lt. Marshall, 2 Lt Conner and 2 Lt. Knowles to Croix to train for Lockleritho. W.J.	

WAR DIARY
or
INTELLIGENCE SUMMARY.

Army Form C. 2118.

Place	Date	Hour	Summary of Events and Information	Remarks and references to Appendices
HERSEAUX	15/11/18		Weather fine. Coys carried out training from 8.900 - 12.30 hours. Recreational games in the afternoon. Lt. Hardcastle returned from leave.	
do	16/11/18		Weather fine. Coys carried out 3 hours training. Capt Mackenzie with Lt Wilmot M.C. & 9 Other Ranks with two lorries proceeded to TOURCOING for Divl Army Thanksgiving Service. Major Keadie M.C. returned from leave & took over duties of 2nd in Command. Capt Mackenzie took over command of "B" Coy. Capt Chisholm took over command of "B" Coy.	
do	17/11/18		Weather fine but cold. Bn. paraded for Divine Service at 10.00 hours. Lieutenant nurse Capt Mackenzie returned. Lt Mengies joined Batt. now posted to "A" Coy.	

Army Form C. 2118.

WAR DIARY
or
INTELLIGENCE SUMMARY.
(Erase heading not required.)

Instructions regarding War Diaries and Intelligence Summaries are contained in F. S. Regs., Part II. and the Staff Manual respectively. Title pages will be prepared in manuscript.

Place	Date	Hour	Summary of Events and Information	Remarks and references to Appendices
HERSEAUX	18/11/18		Weather dull & cold, with slight drizzle of rain. Corp Carried out 3 hours training	
do.	19/11/18		Weather dull & rain. Corp Carried out 3 hours training. Recreational games in the afternoon. Corp for Ultimate started.	
do.	20/11/18		Weather dull, went foggy. Corp Carried out training from 0900 - 1200 hours. Recreational training in the afternoon.	
do.	21/11/18		Weather rained much. Bde. paraded at 0830 hours for rehearsal of Brigade Inspection. Games in the afternoon. Lt. Chalmers reported to Bott. from Hospital.	
do.	22/		Weather cold but fine. Corp carried out 3 hours training in the morning. Games in the afternoon. Lt. Cherbrooke reported for duty of Bde.	

Army Form C. 2118.

Nov. 1918

WAR DIARY
or
INTELLIGENCE SUMMARY.
(Erase heading not required.)

Instructions regarding War Diaries and Intelligence Summaries are contained in F. S. Regs., Part II. and the Staff Manual respectively. Title pages will be prepared in manuscript.

Place	Date	Hour	Summary of Events and Information	Remarks and references to Appendices
BERGEAUX	23/11/18		Weather cold but fine. Batt paraded at 09.00 hours for Bde inspection by Corps Commander.	lel.
do.	24/11/18		Weather cold but fine. Sunday. Batt paraded for Divine Service at 10.00 hours. Lt Clark reported from TI Army School. Lt Cleveland proceeded to Rest Camp PARIS PLAGE.	lel.
do	25/11/18		Weather dull. Coy. Comd's and Platoon training in the morning. Recreational games in the afternoon. Cadres leaving refresher from leave.	lel.
do.	26/11/18		Weather dull. Coys carried out 1½ hours training. Baths at HERBEAUX were allotted to Batt. Class in Theory of Agriculture started.	lel.
do.	27/11/18		Weather dull. Coys carried out 3 hours training. Recreational games in the afternoon.	lel.

Army Form C. 2118.

WAR DIARY
or
INTELLIGENCE SUMMARY.

(Erase heading not required.)

Nov. 1918

Place	Date	Hour	Summary of Events and Information	Remarks and references to Appendices
HERSEAUX	28/11/18		Weather wet. Batt. paraded at 0900 hours for route march. 90 O.R. proceeded on horses to TOURCOING for a lecture on "Exploration in North of India" by Sir J. Younghusband.	WK
do.	29/11/18		Weather fine. Coys carried out training from 0900 — 1200 hours. 80 O.R. proceeded to TOURCOING for lecture on "Demobilisation and Reconstruction." Sport in the afternoon. 2 Lt. CONNELL & 27 O.R. joined Batt.	Coy
do	30/11/18		Weather fine. Coys carried out 3 hours training in the forenoon. Recreational games in the afternoon. 2 Lts ANGUS and 2 Lt JAMIESON proceeded on PARIS leave.	WK

Secret

Volume No. XXX

Army Form W.3091.

Cover for Documents.

Nature of Enclosures.

WAR DIARY

OF THE

14ᵗʰ BATTN ARG. & SUTH'D. HIGHRS.

FOR THE MONTH OF

DECEMBER 1918.

[signature]
Lt. Col.
Comdg. 14ᵗʰ Bn. Arg. & Suth'd. Hrs.

4ᵗʰ January. 1919

Notes, or Letters written.

WAR DIARY
or
INTELLIGENCE SUMMARY.

Army Form C. 2118.

Dec. 1918

Place	Date	Hour	Summary of Events and Information	Remarks and references to Appendices
Fresnoy	1/12/18		Weather fine. Battalion paraded for Divine Service at 1000 hours. Gen. McCracken thanked all parties from leave.	
"	2/12/18		Weather dull. Coys carried out 3 hours training in the forenoon. Recreational training in the afternoon.	
"	3/12/18		Weather dull & showery. Coys carried out 3 hours training. Baths allotted to Coys.	
"	4/12/18		Weather dull. Coys carried out 3 hours training. Part of forecast some Battalion 1st hours boring completion at Fourcaing.	
"	5/12/18		Weather fine. Barrister Lieut. Macd. and Lieut. Gunstetter Lieut. & Col. D. Mackinnon awarded Croix de Guerre (Coys Star) Lt. Lynch assume of Wetter Vicegrd. Lt. Kennedy Viceve up in Cum's weight.	
"	6/12/18		Weather dull. During completion of 3 hours training carried out in the forenoon.	

WAR DIARY
or
INTELLIGENCE SUMMARY

14th Argyll & Sutherland Highlanders
Army Form C. 2118.

Place	Date	Hour	Summary of Events and Information	Remarks and references to Appendices
Helsaut	7/4/18		Weather dull. Bde. H Division inspected the 14th Infantry Brigade. His Knock out Association Football Competition 14th Infantry Brigade 16th Battn. Manchester Regt. Boys came out 3 hours having in the forenoon.	
	8/4/18		Weather showery but cleared up in the afternoon. Rain paraded for Divine Service at 10.00 hours battery 14th I.B. Purple & Corps Labour Group at Association Football. Weather fair. Companies cleaning up. Inventional games in the afternoon. Grenadiers formed Battn with draft of 3 Off.	
	9th		Weather fair with showers. Army Commanders Inspection at Mouveaut. "C" Company reformed the Battalion from torchlight tattoo party.	
	10th			
	11th		Weather showery. Companies carried out a form training. Spent remainder of forenoon cleaning up. 16 Cup v. 16 Papua 16th Manchester at Association Football. 3 miles proceeded for Demobilization.	

Army Form C. 2118.

WAR DIARY
or
INTELLIGENCE SUMMARY.
(Erase heading not required)

14th Argyll & Sutherland Highlanders   Dec 1918

Place	Date	Hour	Summary of Events and Information	Remarks and references to Appendices
HERSEAUX	13/12/18		Weather dull. Coys carried out 2 hours Kennel 2 hours "Manoeuvres". Allowed the Rector from the Gas Depot. 2 hours P.T. Drill. Coys proceed for Demobilization.	
	14/12/18		Weather fair. Coys carried out 2 hours training. Baths allotted to Coys. 2 hours Schooling & inspection. 7 Muirs proceed for Demobilization.	
	15/12/18		Weather fair. Coys carried out 2 hours training. 7 Muirs proceed for Demobilization.	
	16/12/18		Battalion paraded for Divine Service at 1000 hours. Weather dull. 9 Muirs proceed for Demobilization.	
	16/12/18		Weather fair. Coys carried out 2 hours training. 4 Muirs proceed for Demob.	
	17/12/18		Weather dull. Coys carried out 2 hour training. Rugby football match W. M. Coy v 16 Bracketers. 4 Muirs proceed for Demob.	
	18/12/18		Weather showery. Coys carried out 2 hours training. Iron Rations withdrawn from the men.	

Army Form C. 2118
Dec 1918

Instructions regarding War Diaries and Intelligence
Summaries are contained in F. S. Regs., Part II.
and the Staff Manual respectively. Title pages
will be prepared in manuscript.

14th Argyll & Sutherland Highlanders

WAR DIARY
or
INTELLIGENCE SUMMARY.
(Erase heading not required.)

Place	Date	Hour	Summary of Events and Information	Remarks and references to Appendices
HARBARCQ	19/11/18		Weather showery. Coys carried out 2 hours Training. Baths available to Coys	
	20/11/18		Weather fair with showers. Battalion paraded for Battalion Route March. Recreational games in the afternoon.	
	21/11/18		Weather dull. Coys carried out 2 hours Training & Lewis gunner baths.	
	22/11/18		Weather fair. Battalion paraded for Divnl. troops service at 1000 hours	
	23/11/18		Weather dull. Coys carried out 2 hours training.	
	24/11/18		Rain with high wind. Companies carried out shower training. Musketry Drivers.	
	25/11/18		Weather fine. General Holiday.	
	26/11/18		Weather fair with high wind. Battalion paraded at 0930 hours for Battalion Route March	
	27/11/18		Weather showery with high wind. Training carried out in Polish as far as possible.	

Army Form C. 2118.

WAR DIARY
or
INTELLIGENCE SUMMARY.

14th Argyll & Sutherland Highlanders.   Dec 1917

(Erase heading not required.)

Instructions regarding War Diaries and Intelligence Summaries are contained in F. S. Regs., Part II. and the Staff Manual respectively. Title pages will be prepared in manuscript.

Place	Date	Hour	Summary of Events and Information	Remarks and references to Appendices
Meteren	28/7/18		Weather fine. 2 hour Parade at Recreation Ground in the afternoon. 3 rounds of Drill Demonstration Practised for Sunday. Another showery. Battalion Parade for Divine Service at 11:00	
	29/7/18		hours.	
	30/7/18		Weather fair but overcast. Both carried out 2 hours Training. A.M. Football Match. 28 Midd'x Regt versus 14th Arg & Suth'd Ho. Rs. in the Bn League.	
	31/7/18		Hoegenaker Heather fair. 2 hours Training carried out by Companies. Tropps Cross Miller proposed hasen from Senior Officers. Brevde, awarded.	

Secret   Army Form W.3091.

Cover for Documents.

Nature of Enclosures.

War Diary
of the
11th Batn Argyll & Sutherland Highlanders
for the month of
January 1919.

7th February 1919   [signature] Lieut. Col.
                                     Comdg. 14th Bn A&SH

Notes, or Letters written.

WAR DIARY
or
INTELLIGENCE SUMMARY.

Army Form C. 2118.

(Erase heading not required.)

Place	Date	Hour	Summary of Events and Information	Remarks and references to Appendices
Aldershot	18 Jan 1919		Weather stormy. Annual Holiday. Battalion Concert followed by a Dance.	
	21		Weather fine. Companies carried out 3 hours Training. Football Match Sgts. v. N.C.Os. & R. Rank. 3 other ranks discharged.	
	30		Weather showery. Companies carried out 3 hours Training.	
	4th		Weather fair. Battalion Route March at 09.30 hours. Lieut. C.D. Jameson Wilkinson evacuated to hospital. Officers & drafts of 3 immune Dysentery moved as bodyguard. (T. Rodin, M. H. Hall, Verrier, M. Culley, Ruthos Jnr. (2nd Lieut (Acting Capt) Foot (Base)) Lieut. L. Stewart moved from Rouen, Lieut. R. Athey moved from Etaples.	
	5th		Weather Dull. Addition draft for Rouen Known at 11.30 hours. 3 Other Ranks proceeded for Disinfection. Major John Fennell proceeded on leave. Capt. Joll, McKenzie, Gordon etc. proceeded to senior officers' course. Aldershot assembling 13th Jan. Lt. Col. Forsyth took over command of Bn. Coy.	

WAR DIARY
or
INTELLIGENCE SUMMARY.

(Erase heading not required.)

Army Form C. 2118.

Place	Date	Hour	Summary of Events and Information	Remarks and references to Appendices
Aldershot	5/1/19		Lieut. J. Russi Gordon M.C. proceeded to U.K.	AR
	6/1/19		Weather fair. Two Companies carried out 3 hours Training. 14 soldiers with 2 years service declined leave proceeded home to-day.	AR
	7/1/19		Weather fair. Companies carried out 3 hours Training. Rollers allotted Companies to test Machineguns proceeded on final range Kadir M.G. took over range. Lieutenant of Battn. Capt. A.F. Dunston Range proceeded on leave. Medical Charge taken over by Major J.R.B. Gunhlaus.	AR
	8/1/19		Weather fair. Coys carried out 3 hours Training. Lieut. Yorkence Hatch M.C. and Chas. V. 15th (reqd) North Lancs Regt.	AR
	9/1/19		Weather showery. Battalion Training bucketed. Training carried out as found as troops 90 other Ranks proceeded for demobilization under 2/Lieut. E.I. Mackie. Sand hon Lieut. D.C. MILLER proceeded on leave.	AR

Army Form C. 21

WAR DIARY
or
INTELLIGENCE SUMMARY.
(Erase heading not required.)

Instructions regarding War Diaries and Intelligence Summaries are contained in F. S. Regs., Part II. and the Staff Manual respectively. Title pages will be prepared in manuscript.

Place	Date	Hour	Summary of Events and Information	Remarks and references to Appendices
Herseaux	10/1/19		Weather fair. Battalion paraded at 0930 hours for Battalion route march.	JK
	11/1/19		Weather fair. Coys carried out 2 hours training. Brig. Genl Montheau Meter 16th Marching V. U. King Sixth, also 2 Other Ranks proceeded for Demobilization. Sergeants Garb a Victory Dance to the Battalion. Lance Corporal Lihaus awarded Belgian Croix de Guerre.	JK
	12/1/19		Weather dull. Battalion paraded for Divine Service at 1030 hours. Other ranks proceeded for demobilization.	JK
	13/1/19		Weather fair. Companies carried out 3 hours training. 2/Lt Y.G. Blackie home from sick leave. 2/Lt Alderton + 2/Lt D. Wrong proceeded on leave.	JK
	14/1/19		Weather fine. Coys carried out 2 hours training. Baths allotted to Coys.	JK
	15/1/19		Weather fair. Companies carried out 2 hours training.	JK
	16/1/19		Weather fair. Battalion paraded for Battalion Route march at 0930 hours. Capt Little Keagan & 2/Lt Y.G. Haskin proceeded on leave.	JK

WAR DIARY or INTELLIGENCE SUMMARY

Army Form C. 2118.

Place	Date	Hour	Summary of Events and Information	Remarks and references to Appendices
Iroadi	17/1/19		Weather fair. Companies carried out Throwing training	
	18/1/19		Weather fair. Companies carried out 2 hours training. Bayonet Fighting & other exercises. Draft left from S.D.B. London League 9/1/19. Other drafts proceeded for Demobilisation	
	19/1/19		Battalion parade for Divine Service at 10.00 hours. Weather fair. Field King returned from leave.	
	20/1/19		Weather fair. Coys carried out 2½ hours training. Bayo ... etc. Other drafts proceeded for Demobilisation.	
	21/1/19		Weather fair frosty. Baths allotted to Battalion. Lieut. Col. A.O. Bulcher proceeded on leave. Capt A.O. Bulcher proceeded on leave. 9 other ranks proceeded for Demobilisation.	
	22/1/19		Weather fair. Coys carried out 2 hours training. Lieut T.J. Mewges and 15 other ranks proceeded for Demobilisation.	

WAR DIARY
or
INTELLIGENCE SUMMARY.

(Erase heading not required.)

Army Form C. 2118.

Place	Date	Hour	Summary of Events and Information	Remarks and references to Appendices
ROUBAIX	23/1/19		Another heavy frost. Notification received out rehearsal for presentation of colours at Roubaix on 25th inst. A/Cook W. Moore trans. from "A" Coy. Until other Venue was Field Ambulance. Pte. W. Anyswith admitted. Rougaté League (42nd).	
	24/1/19		Weather has cold. Colour Guard. Staff of 3 other ranks, & 3 x other ranks per Company proceeded for rehearsal of Presentation of colours. Lt. Col. A. Mackinnon V.D. handed Mixed talk from leave & took over command of Battalion.	
	25/1/19		Weather keen cold. Presentation of King's Colours at Roubaix at 1100 hours. Major Mullin a/b OR proceeded for demobilization.	
	26/1/19		Weather cold. Snow fell during the night & continued to fall during the day. Battalion paraded for Divine Service at 1000 hours It other Ranks Demobbed.	

WAR DIARY
or
INTELLIGENCE SUMMARY.

(Erase heading not required.)

Army Form C. 2118.

Place	Date	Hour	Summary of Events and Information	Remarks and references to Appendices
Iserlohn	27/1/19		Weather poor. Snow still lying on the ground. Maps to G.S. & U.S. NC & Other ranks proceeded for Rendsburg after training carried out in Huts	
	28/1/19		Weather clear & frosty. Baths allotted to Companies, but ex-worked O/Rks. Other ranks proceeded home for demobilisation	
	29/1/19		Weather clear & frosty. Inst. St. Andries afternoon from leave. Training greatly interfered with on account of condition of roads ground being covered with snow. Lieut R. L. Clemen & 10 Other ranks proceeded home for demobilisation	
	30/1/19		Weather fine frosty. Mj. Stuart & Br. Warning had returned. Battalion. Lieut. Hon. Black Wenyss from ais Riding School. Training carried out in the field	
	31/1/19		Weather frosty. Training carried out in fields.	

Secret

Vol. XXXII
33 φ

(6392) Wt. W6192/P875 1,500,000 4/18 McA & W Ltd (E 2815) Forms W3091/4.   Army Form W.3091.

Cover for Documents.

War Diary.

Nature of Enclosures.

of the

14th Argyll & Sutherland Highlanders

for the month of
Feb. 1919.

[signature]
Lieut Col.
Comdg 14th A & S. Hr.

28.2.19.

Notes, or Letters written.

WAR DIARY
or
INTELLIGENCE SUMMARY.

Army Form C. 2118.

Place	Date	Hour	Summary of Events and Information	Remarks and references to Appendices
Tourcoing	1/2/19		Weather cold. 2 hrs training carried out. "A" Coy amalgamated with "B" Coy to "D" Coy. "E" officer posted to "C" Coy. 21 O.Rs departed for demobilization.	
	2/2/19		Weather fair. Battalion paraded for Divine Service at 1000 hrs. 15 O.Rs demobilised.	
	3/2/19		Weather fair, cold. Boys carried out 2½ hrs training 2/Lt A.W. Jackes rejoined Battn from leave. 43 O.Rs departed for demobilization.	
	4/2/19		Weather cold. Boys carried out 1 hour training. Baths allotted to Battalion.	
	5/2/19		Weather clear, cold. Boys carried out 2½ hrs training. Lt H.S. Miller rejoined Battalion from leave. Lt No. L. Smith joined Battn & posted to "A" Coy.	
	6/2/19		Weather frosty, feelin in Roubaix. Boys carried out 2 hrs training. 2/Lt _____ rejoined unit from leave. 36 O.Rs proceeded for demobilization.	

WAR DIARY
or
INTELLIGENCE SUMMARY

Army Form C. 2118

Place	Date	Hour	Summary of Events and Information	Remarks and references to Appendices
	7/2/19		Weather cold. Lt. A. Benton 2/Lt - A.S. Jamieson rejoined Battalion from leave. Coys carried out Platoon training.	
	8/2/19		Lecture in Fortrance by Town of Okotoks. Weather fair & cold. Coys carried out 2 hrs training.	
	9/2/19		Weather clear & cold. Battalion paraded for Divine service at 10:00 a.m. Capt A. St Paul's on Range afternoon for leave.	
	10/2/19		8 Other ranks to Battalion. Coys sent his training. Boys carried out 2 hr training.	
	11/2/19		Weather cold. Frosty.	
	12/2/19		Weather frosty tongs arrived out 2 hr training.	
	14/2/19		Weather cold. Some snow. Inspection by O.C. Field Ambulance. Coys carried out 2 hr training.	

WAR DIARY
or
INTELLIGENCE SUMMARY.

(Erase heading not required.)

Army Form C. 2118

Place	Date	Hour	Summary of Events and Information	Remarks and references to Appendices
	16/2/19		Divine Service in Concert Hall at 10.00 hrs. Weather cold.	
	18/2/19		Weather cold. 10 ORs applied for demobilization.	
	19/2/19		Weather cold. Draft of 23 ORs proceeded to 2nd Bn. A.I.F. (End of quotation) left Sevenoaks at 0800 hrs.	
	20/2/19		Weather cold. 13 ORs proceeded for demobilization.	
	21/2/19		Weather fine, mild. 11 ORs proceeded to 10 Ondre for Demobilization.	
	23/2/19		Weather fine. 1 OR proceeded for demobilization.	
	24/2/19		Weather fair.	
	25/2/19		Some rain. Bn. Allotted Baths.	

Army Form C. 2118.

WAR DIARY
or
INTELLIGENCE SUMMARY.
(Erase heading not required.)

Instructions regarding War Diaries and Intelligence Summaries are contained in F. S. Regs., Part II. and the Staff Manual respectively. Title pages will be prepared in manuscript.

Place	Date	Hour	Summary of Events and Information	Remarks and references to Appendices
	26/2/19		Bright. Some rain.	
	27/2/19		Weather. Dull.	
	28/2/19		Weather: Unsettled. Some rain. Weekly inspection by O.C. Field Ambulance. 3 O.R.s proceeded for Demobilization.	

Secret   Vol XXXIII

War Diary.
of the.

14th Argyll & Sutherland Highlanders

For the month of March 1919.

31/3/19.

                        Lieut. Colonel.
               Comdg. 14th Argyll & Sutherland Highlanders.

Army Form C. 2118

WAR DIARY
or
INTELLIGENCE SUMMARY.

(Erase heading not required.)

Instructions regarding War Diaries and Intelligence Summaries are contained in F. S. Regs., Part II. and the Staff Manual respectively. Title pages will be prepared in manuscript.

Place	Date	Hour	Summary of Events and Information	Remarks and references to Appendices
Kirkcaldy	1/3/19		Weather fine. Party of 23 other ranks departed from Markinch Station at 6 am to join 2nd Battalion Argyll & Sutherland Highlanders at Hawick.	
do	2/3/19		Weather fine — Church Parade.	
do	3/3/19		Weather dull, a little rain during forenoon. Party of 4 other ranks proceeded to UK for demobilization. 2 Lieut G.J. Mackie proceeded to report to DADRT Boulogne for duty.	
do	4/3/19		Weather fine — Baths allotted to Battalion today.	
do	5/3/19		Weather fine. 2 other ranks returned from demobilization camp. Awarded 28 days FP No. 2.	
do	6/3/19		Weather stormy. Nil.	
do	7/3/19		Weather stormy. Nil.	
do	8/3/19		Weather wet. Nil.	

Army Form C. 2118

WAR DIARY
or
INTELLIGENCE SUMMARY.

(Erase heading not required.)

Instructions regarding War Diaries and Intelligence Summaries are contained in F. S. Regs., Part II. and the Staff Manual respectively. Title pages will be prepared in manuscript.

Place	Date	Hour	Summary of Events and Information	Remarks and references to Appendices
Montecourt	9/3/19		Weather fine. Church Parades. 2nd Lieut J M Ross proceeded to St Andre demobilization centre to conduct demobilization party to U.K.	
do	10/3/19		Weather showery. Nothing of importance happened.	
do	11/3/19		Weather dull. Baths allotted to Battalion today	
do	12/3/19		Weather fine	Nil
do	13/3/19		Weather fine	Nil
do	14/3/19		Weather fine	Nil
do	15/3/19		Weather fine	Nil
do	16/3/19		Weather fine. Lieut M.H. Falls rejoined Battalion from leave.	
do	17/3/19		Weather wet. Drawrides inspected Lewis Guns and Rifles of Battalion	
do	18/3/19		Weather wet. Baths allotted to Battalion today	
do	19/3/19		Weather fine. Lieuts Monahan & Smith 2nd Lieuts McEwing and McRae proceeded to join 5th Battalion Argyll Sutherland Highlanders	

Army Form C. 2118

WAR DIARY
or
INTELLIGENCE SUMMARY.
(Erase heading not required.)

Instructions regarding War Diaries and Intelligence Summaries are contained in F. S. Regs., Part II. and the Staff Manual respectively. Title pages will be prepared in manuscript.

Place	Date	Hour	Summary of Events and Information	Remarks and references to Appendices
Roubaix	21/3/19		Weather fine. 2nd Lieut Council proceeded to St Andre demobilization centre to conduct demobilization party to UK	
do	22/3/19		Weather fine. Nothing of importance	
do	22/3/19		Weather fine. Lieut M.A.Hill, Lieut Lewis, Lieut R.Athey, Capt R.McLeod proceeded on 4 days leave to Brussels etc	
do	23/3/19		Weather fine. Coys Commanders ensured personal kits to met Battalion Commanders. 2nd Lt Mackenzie attached Lieut E.P.Mackie joined	
do	24/3/19		Weather. Raining. Leaving 21 miles east to Annual Camp Tourcoing	
do	25/3/19		Weather. Raining. Baths allotted to Battalion to-day Lieut M.A.Hill, Lt Lewis Lt R.Athey & Capt R.McLeod rejoined Battalion	
do	26/3/19		Weather cold — wet	
do	27/3/19		Snowing. Nothing of importance.	
do	28/3/19		Weather stormy. 1 other rank proceeded to Marseilles for duty Lieut Rochester, Lieut A.Smeller, 2nd Lt Rankin, Lieut M.A.Hill proceeded U.K. for demobilization.	

Army Form C. 2118

WAR DIARY
or
INTELLIGENCE SUMMARY.
(Erase heading not required.)

Place	Date	Hour	Summary of Events and Information	Remarks and references to Appendices
Persaul	29/3/19		Weather cold, frosty	
do	3/5/19		Weather cold, showery	
do	3/31/19		Weather fine. Went E.Y.Wickes and 4 other ranks proceeded to UK for demobilization.	

Secret.   Vol. XXXIV

War Diary

of the

14th Argyll & Sutherland Highlanders.

For the month of April 1919.

[signature] Capt for.
Comdg. 14th Argyll & Sutherland Highlanders

30.4.19.

Army Form C. 2118

WAR DIARY
or
INTELLIGENCE SUMMARY.
(Erase heading not required.)

Instructions regarding War Diaries and Intelligence Summaries are contained in F. S. Regs., Part II. and the Staff Manual respectively. Title pages will be prepared in manuscript.

Place	Date	Hour	Summary of Events and Information	Remarks and references to Appendices
Musama	1/4/19		Weather fine. Baker attested to Battalion.	
	2/4/19		Weather fair. Cold. 1 O.R. proceeded to U.K. on leave.	
	3/4/19		Weather fine. Mild. NIL	
	4/4/19		Weather fine. 1 O.R. rejoined unit from leave.	
	5/4/19		Weather fine. NIL	
	6/4/19		Weather fine. Breezy. NIL	
	7/4/19		Weather fine. Lieut Col P. Mackenzie proceeded to U.K. on leave.	
	8/4/19		Weather fine. Dull. 1 O.R. proceeded on Shanis leave to U.K. Baker attested to Battalion.	

Army Form C. 2117

WAR DIARY
or
INTELLIGENCE SUMMARY.
(Erase heading not required.)

Instructions regarding War Diaries and Intelligence Summaries are contained in F. S. Regs., Part II. and the Staff Manual respectively. Title pages will be prepared in manuscript.

Place	Date	Hour	Summary of Events and Information	Remarks and references to Appendices
Warsaw	9.4.19		Weather fine. 2 O.Rs proceeded to Dismal Centre at Andle for demobilization	
	10.4.19		Weather fine. 1 O.R. proceeded on leave	
	11.4.19		Weather dull. Nil	
	12.4.19		Weather stormy. Wet. 1 O.R. proceeded to St Andle Station preceding on leave	
	13.4.19		Weather unsettled. Nil	
	14.4.19		Weather wet. 1 O.R. proceeded on leave.	
	15.4.19		Advance of Batt. to Battalion	

Army Form C.2118

WAR DIARY
or
INTELLIGENCE SUMMARY.
(Erase heading not required.)

Instructions regarding War Diaries and Intelligence Summaries are contained in F. S. Regs., Part II. and the Staff Manual respectively. Title pages will be prepared in manuscript.

Place	Date	Hour	Summary of Events and Information	Remarks and references to Appendices
Havency	16.4.19		Last 3 br. Q. was proceeded to U.K. on leave	
	17.4.19		Weather fine. One O.R. proceeded on leave	
	18.4.19		Nil	
	19.4.19		Weather fine. 2/O. Soy. fined from purity at 9 mps. Camp at Auchie & 0% proceeded 1/2 from the house at Auchie for inspection	
	20.4.19		Weather bright & cold. Escaped prisoner of War (German) recaptured in Havencux	
	21.4.19		Weather fine. Nil	
	22.4.19		Weather fine. F.G.C.M. held at Havencourt for the bravery of W/s allotted to Unit	

Army Form C.2118

WAR DIARY
or
INTELLIGENCE SUMMARY.

(Erase heading not required.)

Instructions regarding War Diaries and Intelligence Summaries are contained in F. S. Regs., Part II. and the Staff Manual respectively. Title pages will be prepared in manuscript.

Place	Date	Hour	Summary of Events and Information	Remarks and references to Appendices
Huzard	23/4/19		Arrived at Huzard by tug to extend leaving Bruges under 2/Lt to attey. Weather fine	
	24/4/19		Weather fine. NIL	
	25/4/19		Weather fine. 10 men on pass returned	
	26/4/19		Weather fine. Some rain	
	27/4/19		2 O.R's proceeded on leave	
	28/4/19		Weather cold. Some snow. NIL	
	29/4/19		Batch allotted to Batt. Weather cold. Some rain. 4 O.R's proceeded on leave	
	30/4/19		Weather breezy. Fair Brigade party left for trip to Ghent.	

Secret.   Vol. XXXIV

War Diary.

of the

14th Bn. Arg & Suth. Highrs.

for the month of May 1919.

_____ Capt for.
Lieut. Colonel.
Comdg. 14th Argyll & Sutherland Highlanders

1.6.19.

WAR DIARY
or
INTELLIGENCE SUMMARY.

(Erase heading not required.)

Army Form C. 2118.

Instructions regarding War Diaries and Intelligence Summaries are contained in F. S. Regs., Part II. and the Staff Manual respectively. Title pages will be prepared in manuscript.

Place	Date	Hour	Summary of Events and Information	Remarks and references to Appendices
Herseaux Belgium	1/5/19		Weather raining some rain. 2 ORs proceeded to Demobilization Centre at St Andre.	
	2/5/19		Weather fair. 1 OR rejoined from hospital. 2 ORs proceeded on leave.	
	3/5/19		Weather fine.	
	4/5/19		Weather fine. 2 ORs rejoined unit from Base Waging Camp.	
	5/5/19		Weather fair.	
	6/5/19		Weather fine. 1 OR rejoined from leave.	
	7/5/19		10 ORs proceed to join 1st ATS HQ at Le Havre. Weather stormy. Brigade Party visited Brussels.	
	8/5/19		Weather fine. Proposed inspection by Major General Ford.	

Army Form C. 2118.

WAR DIARY
or
INTELLIGENCE SUMMARY.
(Erase heading not required.)

Instructions regarding War Diaries and Intelligence Summaries are contained in F. S. Regs., Part II. and the Staff Manual respectively. Title pages will be prepared in manuscript.

Place	Date	Hour	Summary of Events and Information	Remarks and references to Appendices
Murad	9.5.19		Weather fine.	
	10.5.19		Weather fine. 1 O.R. rejoined Battn from leave	
	11.5.19		Weather Wet. Capt. W. Dixon proceeded on leave.	
	12.5.19		Weather fine	
	13.5.19		do — Baths allotted to Unit.	
	14.5.19		Weather Wet. Stormy. 2 ORs rejoined unit from leave.	
	15.5.19		Weather fine. 4 ORs rejoined unit from leave.	
	16.5.19		Weather fine.	
	17.5.19		do	

WAR DIARY
or
INTELLIGENCE SUMMARY.

Army Form C. 2118.

Place	Date	Hour	Summary of Events and Information	Remarks and references to Appendices
Mirmay	19/5/19		Weather fine.	WS
	20/5/19		Baths allotted for use of Batt".	WS
	21/5/19		Weather fine. 6 ORs departed for Army of Occupation. (2nd & 5th Inniskillings)	WS
	22/5/19		Weather fine. 1 O.R. reported from leave.	WS
	23/5/19		Weather fine.	WS
	24/5/19		Weather fine.	WS
	27/5/19		Lieut. M. Alley proceed to St André on leave. Weather fine. Baths allotted to Batt".	WS
	28/5/19		Weather fine.	WS

Army Form C. 2118.

WAR DIARY
or
INTELLIGENCE SUMMARY.
(Erase heading not required.)

Instructions regarding War Diaries and Intelligence Summaries are contained in F. S. Regs., Part II. and the Staff Manual respectively. Title pages will be prepared in manuscript.

Place	Date	Hour	Summary of Events and Information	Remarks and references to Appendices
Roisel	29/5/19		Capt. W. Simon Morrice Macdonald returned from leave and proceeded on sub-investigation. Weather fine	|||
	30/5/19		Weather fine	|||
	31/5/19		Weather fine	|||

Secret. Vol XXXVI 379

War Diary

of

14th Argyll & Sutherland Highlanders.

for

Month of June 1919.

R. A____ Lieut
Comdg. 14th Argyll & Sutherland Highlanders.

Desat.

Doc XXXVI

Class visat

Book of Issue 1919

Army Form C. 2118.

WAR DIARY
or
INTELLIGENCE SUMMARY.
(Erase heading not required.)

Instructions regarding War Diaries and Intelligence Summaries are contained in F. S. Regs., Part II. and the Staff Manual respectively. Title pages will be prepared in manuscript.

Place	Date	Hour	Summary of Events and Information	Remarks and references to Appendices
Herseaux	1st to 6th June		Cadre billeted in Herseaux. Orders received for Cadre to proceed to UK for dispersal. Lieut. DM of Weir in charge of Colour Party proceeded to Brighton with Cadre on 6/6/19. Equipment Guard of 2 Officers & 12 O.R's hands remained in Herseaux with all Mobilization Equipment Re.	

R. A. Murray Lieut.
Comdg 1/4th Bn A.S.H. Cadre.

14TH DIVISION
42ND INFY BDE

9TH BN K.R.R.C.
MAY 1915 - JUN 1918

Disbanded 3.8.18

www.ingramcontent.com/pod-product-compliance
Lightning Source LLC
Chambersburg PA
CBHW081359160426
43193CB00013B/2063